Three Mile Island

GREAT DISASTERS
REFORMS and RAMIFICATIONS

Three Mile Island

Therese DeAngelis

CHELSEA HOUSE PUBLISHERS
Philadelphia

Frontispiece: The words spray-painted on this bed sheet express the joy and relief felt not only by Pennsylvanians but also by the entire nation.

> *Dedication:* This book is dedicated to the people of south-central Pennsylvania, especially my family and friends, who survived the fear and uncertainty of the Three Mile Island disaster.

CHELSEA HOUSE PUBLISHERS
Editor in Chief Sally Cheney
Director of Production Kim Shinners
Production Manager Pamela Loos
Art Director Sara Davis
Production Editor Diann Grasse

Staff for THREE MILE ISLAND
Senior Editor John Ziff
Layout 21st Century Publishing and Communications, Inc.

© 2002 by Chelsea House Publishers, a subsidiary of Haights Cross Communications. All rights reserved. Printed and bound in the United States of America.

First Printing

1 3 5 7 9 8 6 4 2

The Chelsea House World Wide Web address is
http://www.chelseahouse.com

CIP applied for ISBN 0-7910-5785-2

Contents

Introduction
Jill McCaffrey   7

1 A Glassful of Water   11

2 "Too Cheap to Meter"   17

3 Turnkey Plants and
         the China Syndrome   31

4 Thirty Minutes to Meltdown   41

5 "An Incident of Some Moment"   55

6 "The World Has Never Known
         a Day Quite Like Today"   73

7 A Legacy of Fear   91

8 What the Future Holds   111

Chronology   116
Further Reading   120
Index   122

GREAT DISASTERS
REFORMS and RAMIFICATIONS

THE *APOLLO 1* AND *CHALLENGER* DISASTERS

BHOPAL

THE BLACK DEATH

THE BLIZZARD OF 1888

THE BOMBING OF HIROSHIMA

THE CHERNOBYL NUCLEAR DISASTER

THE DUST BOWL

THE EXPLOSION OF TWA FLIGHT 800

THE *EXXON VALDEZ*

THE GALVESTON HURRICANE

THE GREAT CHICAGO FIRE

THE GREAT PLAGUE AND FIRE OF LONDON

THE *HINDENBURG*

THE HOLOCAUST

THE INFLUENZA PANDEMIC OF 1918

THE IRISH POTATO FAMINE

THE JOHNSTOWN FLOOD

LOVE CANAL

THE MUNICH OLYMPICS

NUCLEAR SUBMARINE DISASTERS

THE OKLAHOMA CITY BOMBING

PEARL HARBOR

THE SALEM WITCH TRIALS

THE SAN FRANCISCO EARTHQUAKE OF 1906

THE SPANISH INQUISITION

THE STOCK MARKET CRASH OF 1929

TERRORISM

THREE MILE ISLAND

THE *TITANIC*

THE TRIANGLE SHIRTWAIST COMPANY FIRE OF 1911

THE WACO SIEGE

THE WORLD TRADE CENTER BOMBING

Jill McCaffrey
National Chairman
Armed Forces Emergency Services
American Red Cross

Introduction

Disasters have always been a source of fascination and awe. Tales of a great flood that nearly wipes out all life are among humanity's oldest recorded stories, dating at least from the second millennium B.C., and they appear in cultures from the Middle East to the Arctic Circle to the southernmost tip of South America and the islands of Polynesia. Typically gods are at the center of these ancient disaster tales—which is perhaps not too surprising, given the fact that the tales originated during a time when human beings were at the mercy of natural forces they did not understand.

To a great extent, we still are at the mercy of nature, as anyone who reads the newspapers or watches nightly news broadcasts can attest.

INTRODUCTION

Hurricanes, earthquakes, tornados, wildfires, and floods continue to exact a heavy toll in suffering and death, despite our considerable knowledge of the workings of the physical world. If science has offered only limited protection from the consequences of natural disasters, it has in no way diminished our fascination with them. Perhaps that's because the scale and power of natural disasters force us as individuals to confront our relatively insignificant place in the physical world and remind us of the fragility and transience of our lives. Perhaps it's because we can imagine ourselves in the midst of dire circumstances and wonder how we would respond. Perhaps it's because disasters seem to bring out the best and worst instincts of humanity: altruism and selfishness, courage and cowardice, generosity and greed.

As one of the national chairmen of the American Red Cross, a humanitarian organization that provides relief for victims of disasters, I have had the privilege of seeing some of humanity's best instincts. I have witnessed communities pulling together in the face of trauma; I have seen thousands of people answer the call to help total strangers in their time of need.

Of course, helping victims after a tragedy is not the only way, or even the best way, to deal with disaster. In many cases planning and preparation can minimize damage and loss of life—or even avoid a disaster entirely. For, as history repeatedly shows, many disasters are caused not by nature but by human folly, shortsightedness, and unethical conduct. For example, when a land developer wanted to create a lake for his exclusive resort club in Pennsylvania's Allegheny Mountains in 1880, he ignored expert warnings and cut corners in reconstructing an earthen dam. On May 31, 1889, the dam gave way, unleashing 20 million tons of water on the towns below. The Johnstown Flood, the deadliest in American history, claimed more than 2,200 lives. Greed and negligence would figure prominently in the Triangle Shirtwaist Company fire in 1911. Deplorable conditions in the garment sweatshop, along with a failure to give any thought to the safety of workers, led to the tragic deaths of 146 persons. Technology outstripped wisdom only a year later, when the designers of the luxury liner *Titanic* smugly declared their state-of-the-art ship "unsinkable," seeing no need to provide lifeboat capacity for everyone onboard. On the night of April 14, 1912, more than 1,500 passengers and crew paid for this hubris with their lives after the ship collided with an iceberg and sank. But human catastrophes aren't always the unforeseen consequences of carelessness or folly. In the 1940s the leaders of Nazi Germany purposefully and systematically set out to exterminate all Jews, along with Gypsies, homosexuals, the mentally ill, and other so-called undesirables. More recently terrorists have targeted random members of society, blowing up airplanes and buildings in an effort to advance their political agendas.

The books in the GREAT DISASTERS: REFORMS AND RAMIFICATIONS series examine these and other famous disasters, natural and human made. They explain the causes of the disasters, describe in detail how events unfolded, and paint vivid portraits of the people caught up in dangerous circumstances. But these books are more than just accounts of what happened to whom and why. For they place the disasters in historical perspective, showing how people's attitudes and actions changed and detailing the steps society took in the wake of each calamity. And in the end, the most important lesson we can learn from any disaster—as well as the most fitting tribute to those who suffered and died—is how to avoid a repeat in the future.

At 4:00 A.M. on March 28, 1979, residents near Three Mile Island were awakened by a terrible roar. This huge release of steam signaled the beginning of the worst nuclear accident in U.S. history.

A Glassful of Water

Bill Whittock was a retired civil engineer living in Goldsboro, a small town on the west shore of the Susquehanna River in south-central Pennsylvania. Just east of his home, on one of the islands dotting the river, stood a nuclear power plant known as Three Mile Island. TMI, as local residents knew it, was relatively new and had been built in two parts. Unit 1 (called TMI-1), an enormous, 800-megawatt (MW) reactor, had gone into operation in September 1974. Unit 2 (TMI-2), an even larger 900-MW reactor, had taken 10 years to complete and opened in December 1978.

At 4:00 A.M. on March 28, 1979, just three months after TMI-2 started operations, Whittock was awakened by a "terrible roar" like the sound of an airplane taking off. Startled, he went to his bedroom window and looked across the river at the four floodlit cooling towers that loomed 370 feet above the plant, nearly filling the skyline. Spurting out of TMI-2's containment building (the smaller, domed concrete structure housing the nuclear reactor) was a huge jet of steam. "It was narrow when it started," Whittock remembers, "and when it went up it expanded until it was half the width of the towers as it went out over the top." Not far away from Whittock's home, across Route 441 from the plant, Holly Garnish also heard the noise. "Picture the biggest jet at an airport and the sound it makes," she recalled. "That's what I heard. It shook the windows, the whole house."

While the shriek was certainly surprising at that time of the day, it was not the first time residents living along the Susquehanna River had heard such sounds. Since TMI-2 had begun operation, they had heard similar releases numerous times. The Garnishes were so used to it that on this morning Holly's husband, John, slept through it. "[W]ell, this is just another time [the reactor has] gone off over there again!" Whittock remembers telling himself. "I went back to bed."

No one working in Unit 2 paid much attention to the sound either. The plant was always filled with the banging and rushing noises of millions of gallons of water flowing through huge pipes. Like its counterpart, TMI-1, Unit 2 was a pressurized water reactor (PWR), the most common type of nuclear power generator in the United States. In a fossil fuel power plant, coal, oil, natural gas, or a combination of these substances is burned to create enough heat to boil water into steam. The steam in turn propels the blades of a turbine generator to produce electricity. In a PWR, however, the heat to boil the water is produced by bombarding uranium with neutrons. This produces fission (the splitting of atoms) in a carefully controlled chain reaction that releases massive amounts of energy.

The uranium, which is highly radioactive, is stored as checker-sized pellets in zirconium containers called fuel rods, each of which holds hundreds of the pellets. TMI-2 had 36,816 fuel rods in its reactor core—the heart of a nuclear power plant where the atomic reaction takes place. The core was housed in a 40-foot-high pressure vessel with eight-inch-thick steel walls. The pressure vessel in turn was encased in a containment building, a massive concrete structure 190 feet high.

In reactors like TMI-2, the core is always immersed in water. This water, called primary coolant, not only helps slow and control the fission process, but it also transfers the heat produced by fission to the turbines. The water travels through a closed system of pipes, called the primary loop; the pipes run into and out of the reactor core. Since primary coolant is radioactive, it never leaves the pressure vessel or the primary loop. Instead, it transfers heat via steam generators to another system of pipes called the secondary loop or feedwater circuit. The feedwater is the water that turns to steam and drives the turbine. Once it has done its job, the feedwater is cooled via the cooling towers and pumped back to the generators to transfer more heat away from the core.

About an hour before local residents heard the blast of steam on March 28, 1979, third-shift foreman Fred Scheimann and two auxiliary operators were in the secondary loop area of TMI-2, attempting to clean a condensate polisher—one of several tall columns filled with special resin beads that filter impurities from the feedwater. The men tried to pump the beads into a flushing tank, but the resin became blocked in a pipe. This problem happened frequently, but this time the compressed air hose that they normally used to force the pipe clear was not working. Frustrated, Scheimann tried another method. He agitated the water in the bottom of the polisher to create a bubbling mixture of air, water, and resin. It worked; finally, the pipe was clear.

As Scheimann and the auxiliary operators went on to another project, they did not realize that they had left behind

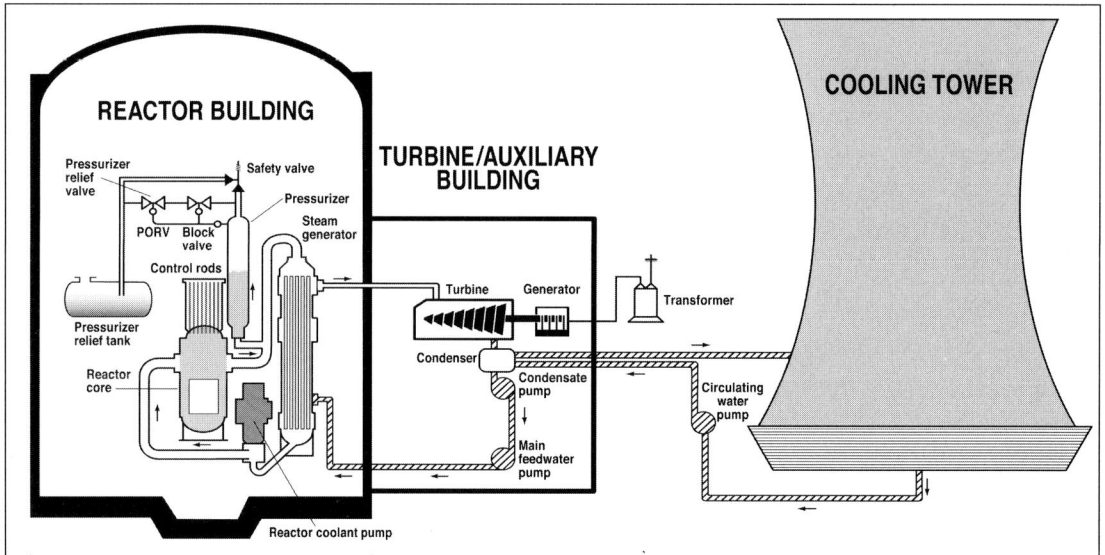

This diagram depicts the three integral parts of a nuclear power plant similar in construction to TMI: the reactor building, containing the pressurized water reactor and the steam generator; the auxiliary building housing the turbines and generators; and the cooling towers.

a small leak. A little less than a glassful of water was snaking through a maze of pipes called the instrument air system, which regulated pneumatic controls throughout the plant and kept air pressure constant in critical areas. Nuclear power plants are by necessity equipped with several layers of backup and safety systems; at TMI, if air pressure was lost or its flow was interrupted, control valves were supposed to engage wherever the problem was detected, opening or closing to prevent malfunctions or dangerous accidents.

When the leak reached the two feedwater pumps, their control valves operated correctly and closed, shutting the pumps down. All throughout the system, other valves automatically slammed shut as a result of the feedwater pump valves closing. One special valve, called the Electromatic relief valve (ERV), was located on the pressurizer, a tank positioned above and beside the reactor vessel. As its name implies, the pressurizer maintains cooling system pressure and water levels, preventing them from rising too high by briefly releasing steam through the ERV into a quench (holding) tank.

At the same time as TMI-2's safety valves engaged, a process called a scram began in its reactor core. In just one second, 69 silver and boron control rods dropped into place among the fuel rods to halt the nuclear chain reaction. Meanwhile, in an adjacent building, the turbine tripped (shut down)—another safety precaution—and a control valve released steam that normally would have been used to generate electricity into the outside air instead. This release created the roar that woke nearby residents that morning.

The equipment was operating as it should have—with one disastrous exception. The ERV on the pressurizer, supposed to remain open for only 13 seconds, malfunctioned and stayed open, allowing primary coolant to continue pouring from the reactor core into the quench tank. In the TMI-2 control room, shift supervisor Bill Zewe and the other operators on duty had no idea that the ERV had stuck open. When they looked at the control panel—a huge, U-shaped double bank of 1,200 dials, warning lights, and vertical gauges—it told them that the valve had closed properly.

Without enough coolant to regulate it, the temperature in the reactor core soared and the steam generators began to boil dry. Backup pumps turned on to restore water flow to the steam generators—but the pumps were prevented from doing so by two other closed valves that were supposed to remain open at all times. In the reactor, the temperature was rising by 40° F per second, eventually reaching a lavalike 5,000° F. At that point, the fuel rods began to melt and sink toward the bottom of the steel casing surrounding the core.

What Bill Whittock, Holly Garnish, and other area residents did not realize is that the blast of steam they heard that morning was the first sign of an unprecedented nuclear disaster at Three Mile Island. A catastrophic series of events, which included operator errors and equipment failure, would combine with poor system design, inconsistent management decisions, and widespread misinformation to lead Pennsylvania—and the entire world—to the brink of a nuclear meltdown.

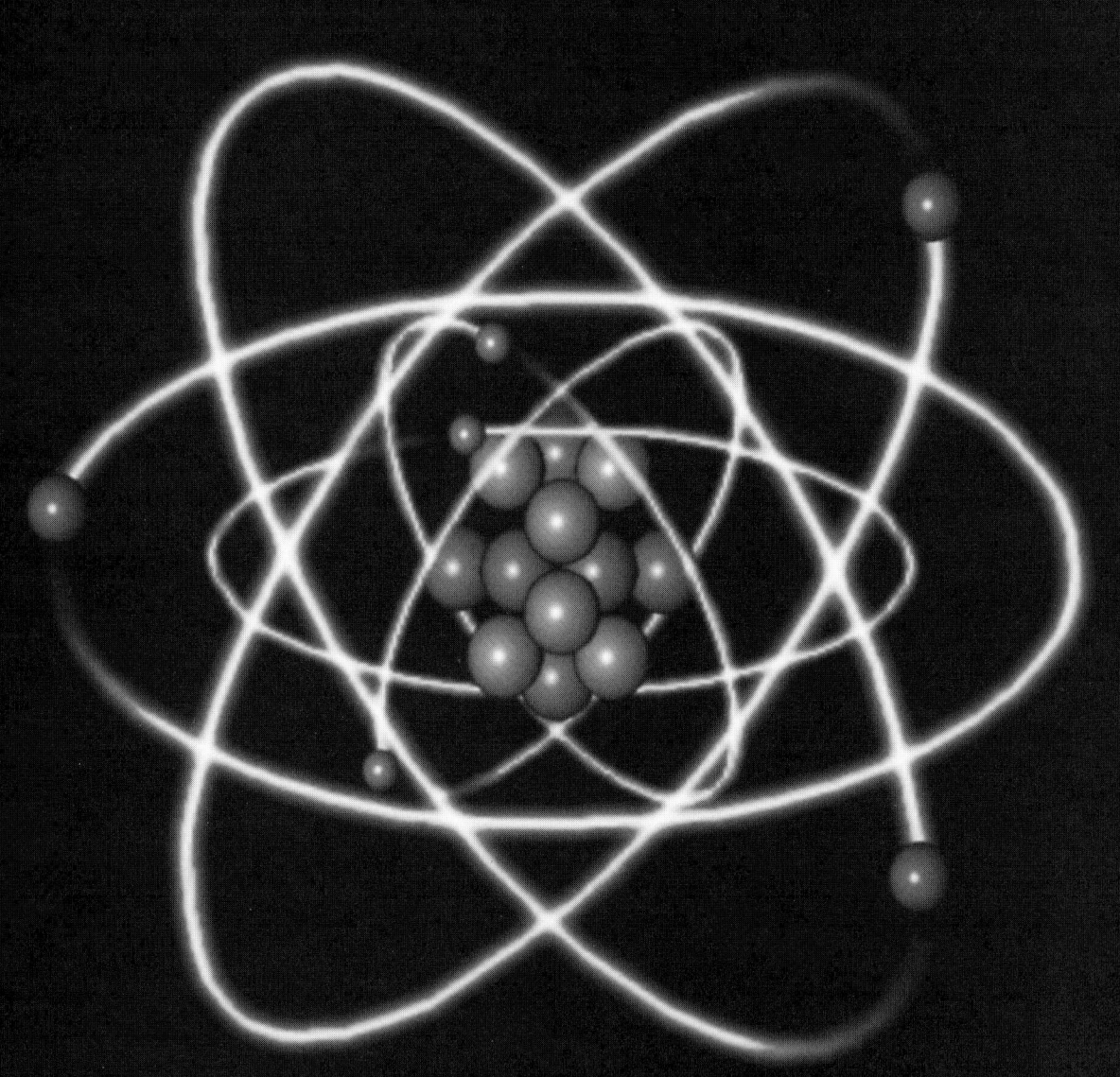

An atom, the smallest whole particle of matter, is composed of three types of particles: protons, neutrons, and electrons. Just as planets orbit the sun, electrons travel in orbits around the nucleus (center) of an atom, which consists of densely packed protons and neutrons.

"Too Cheap to Meter"

In 1895 Wilhelm Roentgen discovered strange rays emanating from certain materials after he bombarded them with electricity. He could not have dreamed that in less than 60 years his findings would lead to nuclear power plants. Roentgen, a German physicist, was not even sure what these mysterious rays were, so he called them x rays. A year later, French physicist Antoine Henri Becquerel discovered that some materials give off x rays without being exposed to electricity. A few years after Becquerel's discovery Marie Curie, a Polish scientist working in France, learned that uranium, a metallic element discovered in 1789, was giving off the x rays Becquerel had noted. Curie called this quality radioactivity. With her husband, Pierre, she also discovered two other radioactive elements: radium and polonium.

What makes a substance radioactive? An atom, the smallest whole particle of matter, is made up of three types of particles: protons, neutrons, and electrons. To imagine the structure of an atom, picture Earth's solar system. Just as planets orbit the sun, electrons travel in orbits around the nucleus (center) of an atom, which consists of densely packed protons and neutrons. Each type of subatomic particle has an electrical charge. Protons, which are positively charged, are attracted to electrons, which have a negative charge. Neutrons, as the name suggests, are neutral and have no charge; they serve as binding agents for protons in the nucleus.

As electrons whirl around a nucleus, they form a cloud of negative charge that is normally balanced by the positive charge of protons. The numbers of electrons and protons in an atom are equal, so the atom itself has no charge. Electrons are responsible for the chemical and electrical properties of matter. The number of protons determines what kind of matter the atom is. For example, an atom with 13 protons and electrons and 14 neutrons is always aluminum.

The sum of the number of neutrons and protons in an atom is called its atomic mass number. It is possible to have several forms of an element with varying atomic mass numbers. These forms are called isotopes. For example, one of the simplest and most common elements, hydrogen, has three isotopes. Of these, hydrogen-3 is an unstable form. Unstable isotopes give off excess energy until they become stable, and in so doing they decay into another element.

Just as gravity keeps the planets orbiting the sun, each atom is held together by the immense energy of opposing electrical forces. When an element decays, the energy it releases is called radioactivity. A radioactive isotope can decay in one of three processes: alpha decay, beta decay, and spontaneous fission. In alpha decay, two protons and two neutrons released from an atom's nucleus form alpha particles. Beta decay occurs when a neutron spontaneously becomes a proton, electron, and another type of particle called an antineutrino. The electron and antineutrino are ejected from the nucleus, leaving the proton. The ejected electron is called a beta particle. Alpha particles have a positive electrical charge and beta particles have a negative charge. The third kind of decay, spontaneous fission, occurs when an atom splits and becomes two atoms rather than throwing off subatomic particles. The rate at which a radioactive element decays is measured as a half-life—the time required for one-half of a given quantity of the element to decay.

The process of generating electricity using nuclear power begins with uranium, which is radioactive in all its isotopes. With a half-life of 4.5 billion years, the isotope uranium-238 is fairly abundant; it makes up 99 percent of all uranium on Earth. The other one percent is either uranium-235 or uranium-234. Uranium-238 and uranium-235 usually undergo alpha decay, but uranium-235 can also decay by fission.

Not long after scientists discovered the nature of atomic decay, they began seeking a way to harness its immense energy. In 1938, German physicists Otto Hahn and Fritz Strassman demonstrated that nuclei of uranium-235 atoms could be forced to undergo fission rather than decay naturally. Four years later, on December 2, 1942, Enrico Fermi, the leader of a team of prominent scientists commissioned by the U.S. government, bombarded the nuclei of uranium-235

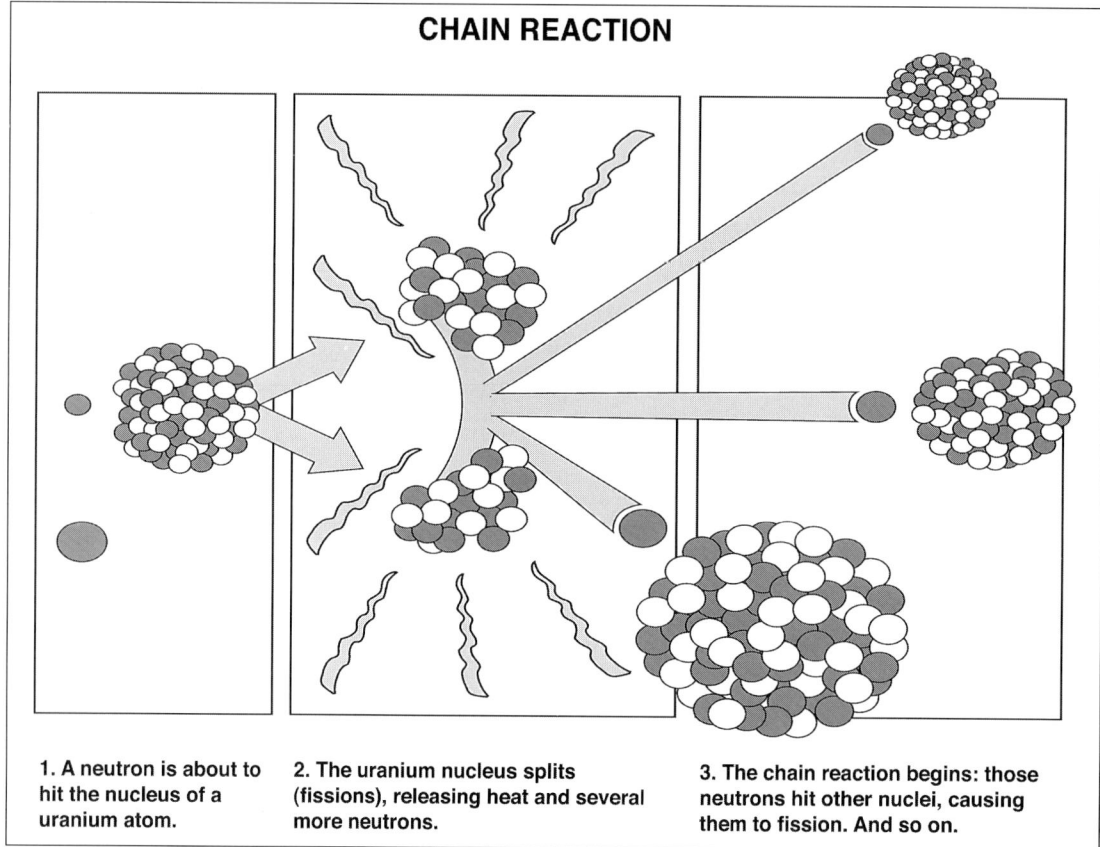

CHAIN REACTION

1. A neutron is about to hit the nucleus of a uranium atom.
2. The uranium nucleus splits (fissions), releasing heat and several more neutrons.
3. The chain reaction begins: those neutrons hit other nuclei, causing them to fission. And so on.

On December 2, 1942, Enrico Fermi, the leader of a team of prominent scientists commissioned by the U.S. government, created the first self-sustained nuclear chain reaction.

atoms with free neutrons. Each of the nuclei immediately split into two lighter atoms, releasing neutrons and protons that in turn bombarded nearby uranium-235 atoms, causing their nuclei to split. Fermi and his colleagues had created the first self-sustained nuclear chain reaction.

Energy is released during a nuclear chain reaction in the form of heat and gamma radiation. Unlike alpha and beta particles, a gamma ray is a kind of high-energy X ray or electromagnetic pulse emitted by "excited" nuclei; these rays often accompany alpha and beta decay. Gamma rays can easily penetrate matter deeply, and they can have extremely adverse effects on animal cells, including those of humans. (Lead, which gamma rays cannot penetrate, is an effective shield against these effects.)

Before uranium can sustain a chain reaction sufficient to fuel a nuclear power plant, it must be enriched. This means that its makeup must be increased from less than one percent (as found in nature) to up to three percent of uranium-235. (By contrast, weapons-grade uranium must be at least 90 percent uranium-235.) Exactly how much energy is released during uranium fission? The power in a pound of enriched uranium, which is smaller than an orange, is equal to the power generated by about one million gallons of gasoline. This much gasoline would fill a building five stories high.

The most important aspect of Enrico Fermi's experiments was to control the nuclear chain reaction to prevent devastating damage. At this point no one knew what consequences would occur from a nuclear explosion or accident, so Fermi and his colleagues built multiple safeguards into their experiment. They assembled a collection of uranium-oxide rods produced by the Westinghouse Company, a commercial energy provider, and embedded them in a pile of graphite blocks. In this array, which Fermi called an atomic pile, they included control rods to fine-tune the reaction and prevent runaway fission. One of these rods was powered by an electric engine and triggered by a radiation monitor. Another was kept out of the pile by a rope with a weight tied to its other end. Should something unexpected occur, a man with an axe stood by to cut the rope and drop the emergency rod into the reaction. The person who had this job was called the safety control rod axe man, and the acronym "scram," used to describe an emergency shutdown in a nuclear power plant, was derived from this term.

Because Fermi's successful testing occurred when much of the world was embroiled in World War II, subsequent research focused on military applications. During the war, the United States, Great Britain, and Canada—members of the Allied Forces—assembled their top scientists in a race to develop an atom bomb before Germany, a member of the Axis Powers, could do so. The research and testing conducted by the top-secret Allied program, called the Manhattan Project, culminated in the atomic bombs that destroyed the Japanese cities of Hiroshima and Nagasaki on August 6 and 9, 1945, respectively. (Germany had surrendered three months earlier, before the first atomic bomb was tested.) The devastating effects of the Hiroshima and Nagasaki bombs ended the war by forcing Japan to surrender.

Despite the incredible devastation caused by atomic weapons, most scientists and many politicians believed that atomic power could be harnessed for peaceful purposes. In December 1945, before a U.S. Congressional committee, nuclear physicist Alvin Weinberg explained the awesome potential of nuclear power: "Atomic power," he said, "can cure as well as kill. It can fertilize and enrich a region as well as devastate it. It can widen man's horizons as well as force him back into the cave."

In the postwar era, countries conducting nuclear experiments no longer had the unifying goal of defeating the enemy in battle. U.S. government officials were wary of trusting potent and promising technology with other nations, even with its allies— but especially with the Soviet Union. In spite of Weinberg's testimony and that of other respected scientists, the U.S. government held a tight rein on nuclear experimentation and kept the focus on military uses.

In 1946 the United States Congress passed the Atomic Energy Act, which replaced the Manhattan Project with the five-member Atomic Energy Commission (AEC). The AEC, a civilian body, was designed to supervise atomic technology research and testing in the United States and to protect the public from its dangers. But the act only mentioned in passing the peacetime uses of nuclear power, and it prohibited privatization of the technology. Not until two years after the Atomic Energy Act was passed was the Advisory Committee on Reactor Safeguards (ACRS) founded. The committee's job was to advise the AEC on the possible safety and design factors inherent in building nuclear reactors for generating electricity.

In 1949, the federal government established the National Reactor Testing Station (NRTS) in Arco, Idaho. There, scientists built and tested several types of nuclear reactors, including the Experimental Breeder Reactor (EBR-I), a so-called fast-breeder reactor that not only generates power but also produces fuel for other reactors; a boiling-water reactor (BWR); a low-power reactor used to test the other designs; and a submarine-thermal reactor. On December 20, 1951, the NRTS produced the first usable electricity ever generated by a nuclear reactor when EBR-I lighted four 150-watt bulbs.

Other countries developed their own programs as well. Great Britain and the Soviet Union in particular conducted testing focused on developing nuclear weapons. A long period of distrust and tension, commonly called the Cold War, developed between the United States and the Soviet Union as a result. In

The federal government established the National Reactor Testing Station (NRTS) in Arco, Idaho. There, scientists built and tested several types of nuclear reactors, including the Experimental Breeder Reactor (EBR-I), shown here. On December 20, 1951, the EBR-I produced the first usable electricity ever generated by a nuclear reactor.

1949, the USSR tested its first atomic bomb, and Great Britain followed three years later. In the United States, many officials believed it was vitally important not to fall behind other nations in the field of nuclear technology, and a race ensued to develop peacetime uses, much like the wartime effort to develop the atomic bomb itself.

The first practical application of nuclear energy in the United States was for military purposes, although it was not a weapon. U.S. Navy captain Hyman Rickover, an enthusiastic proponent of nuclear energy, convinced the Department of Defense to develop a nuclear system that could power an aircraft carrier. Although he succeeded—the Department of Defense approved the project and work began in 1953—officials later decided the cost was prohibitive and canceled the project. Undaunted, Rickover set his sights on a more manageable project: he convinced Westinghouse to establish a laboratory to develop a nuclear reactor that could power a submarine. (The laboratory eventually became the Bettis Atomic Power Laboratory.) On January 21, 1954, the world's first nuclear submarine, the USS *Nautilus*, was completed. *Nautilus* could travel for months without surfacing or refueling. Other nations conducting atomic research rushed to develop similar vessels; Rickover became an admiral and was thereafter known as the father of the nuclear navy.

With this accomplishment in hand, Admiral Rickover appeared before the AEC and the Joint Committee on Atomic Energy to persuade members of the political and commercial necessity of developing a nuclear reactor similar to the one at the NRTS. He argued that although billions of dollars had been spent on nuclear research for military purposes, none had been allotted for peacetime or commercial use. Moreover, Great Britain and the USSR seemed well on their way to winning the race to develop safe nuclear power generators.

Rickover had a high-ranking ally: President Dwight D. Eisenhower. In a December 1953 address to the United Nations, the U.S. president outlined in stark terms the destructive power of nuclear warfare, but emphasized that "this greatest of all destructive forces can be developed into a great boon, for the benefit of all mankind." Many federal officials agreed with Eisenhower, as did a great number of Americans. The arguments were effective. The AEC issued a request for proposals from utility companies and engineering vendors to operate the first nuclear power plant.

Of the nine companies that submitted proposals, the AEC chose the Duquesne Light Company of Pittsburgh, Pennsylvania, which joined contractor Westinghouse and the government-run Bettis Atomic Power Laboratory in the effort. In September 1954, Eisenhower launched the groundbreaking for construction of a nuclear plant in Shippingport, Pennsylvania (near Pittsburgh), by waving an "atomic wand" past a Geiger counter, which signaled an automated bulldozer to begin digging. The Shippingport plant would be built and owned by the U.S. government, but Duquesne would manage and operate it.

In 1954, Congress passed a second Atomic Energy Act, allowing nuclear power to be privatized for commercial use in the United States. "The Atomic Energy Act of [1954] resulted partly from perceptions of the long-range need for new energy sources, but mostly from the immediate commitment to maintain America's world leadership in nuclear technology, enhance its international prestige, and demonstrate the benefits of peaceful atomic energy," says the United States Nuclear Regulatory Commission (NRC) in a brief history of U.S. nuclear power. "It infused the atomic power program with a sense of urgency." Lewis Strauss, the chairman of the AEC, shared the enthusiasm of many scientists and politicians. "It is not too much to expect that our children will enjoy in their home electrical energy too cheap to meter," he declared.

With the new federal law in place, the AEC set about defining regulations for commercial development of nuclear power sources in the United States. The committee was now entrusted not only with

"TOO CHEAP TO METER"

Clinton Anderson (left), Chairman of the Joint Congressional Committee on Atomic Energy, talks with AEC Chairman Lewis Strauss as they examine a photograph of the construction of the Shippingport nuclear power plant.

supervising a federal nuclear weapons program, but also with encouraging the development of peaceful uses for nuclear energy. It would not become clear until years later that these goals conflicted with one another.

AEC members believed that the best way to advance the development of commercial nuclear power was to form partnerships between the federal government and private energy companies. In early 1955 it launched a "power demonstration reactor program," for which the U.S. government agreed to provide research and development in its national laboratories and subsidize further research by private companies. The government still owned all fissionable materials (such as uranium supplies), but it announced that it would waive fuel-use charges for loaning the materials to participating companies. The companies were responsible for supplying the funding for plant construction and for all operating costs. The AEC hoped that the program would encourage power companies to experiment with reactor designs and determine which was most effective.

Although Shippingport was the first nuclear power plant constructed, Pittsburgh was not the first American town to receive all of its electricity from nuclear power. That distinction belongs to Arco, Idaho, where in 1955 the NRTS successfully engineered its boiling-water reactor (BWR), called BORAX III, to provide power to residents. And while Westinghouse was the first company to break ground for the construction of a nuclear power plant, rival General Electric (GE) won the first truly commercial nuclear power plant contract. GE had been involved with the Manhattan Project and had participated in nuclear research and development at the federal government's Argonne National Laboratory in Argonne, Illinois. GE had also contracted with the U.S. government to conduct nuclear power plant research at the Knolls Atomic Power Laboratory in Niskayuna, New York. Although the government retooled the Knolls project to focus on naval propulsion in 1950, GE had attained the nuclear energy technology and experience to compete with Westinghouse.

GE's entry began with the Vallecitos plant in Pleasanton, California. A collaborative effort between

GE and Pacific Gas and Electric Company, Vallecitos was built to test fuel, nuclear core components, and plant controls, and to train personnel to operate a full-scale nuclear power plant. The plant was completed in June 1957 and began producing power in October, when the AEC granted Vallecitos the first U.S. power reactor license. Just two months later, on December 23, 1957, the Shippingport plant reached full power and began providing electricity to Pittsburgh.

> The passage of the 1954 Atomic Energy Act and the introduction of the power demonstration reactor program encouraged private companies to build nuclear power plants.

Turnkey Plants and the China Syndrome

3

As the AEC had hoped, the passage of the 1954 Atomic Energy Act and the introduction of the power demonstration reactor program encouraged private companies to experiment with nuclear reactor designs. Today, three basic types of nuclear power plants exist. The water-cooled reactor, which accounts for 75 percent of reactors in use today, employs water as a coolant and moderator—meaning that water is used to slow down fast-moving neutrons that are produced during the nuclear chain reaction. This allows the neutrons to be captured by other nuclei and keeps the fission process going. The two other types are the fast reactor, which uses liquid metal (usually sodium) as a coolant; and the gas-cooled reactor, which uses helium as a coolant and graphite as a moderator.

The Vallecitos and Shippingport plants both had variations of water-cooled reactors. Vallecitos contained a boiling-water reactor; Shippingport was an early version of a pressurized water reactor—the same design that would be incorporated into Three Mile Island 17 years later. The difference between a PWR and a BWR lies in the way the heat from the core of the reactor is transferred to the turbines. In a BWR, the water directly in contact with the fuel rods is allowed to boil and convert to steam, which then travels to the turbine and produces power through the generator. In a PWR, the reactor is housed in a huge steel tank called the pressure vessel, through which three separate coolant circuits (or loops) run. As in a BWR, these loops move heat via steam from the reactor core to the turbines. However, as the name suggests, water in the core of a PWR is prevented from boiling by means of extremely high pressure—2,250 pounds per square inch (the pressure relief valve prevents excess pressure from bursting the steel tank).

The heat generated by fission is transferred from water in the primary loop (which is in contact with the fuel rods) to the secondary loop (which is never in contact with radioactive materials) via a heat exchanger. The PWR has a number of advantages over the BWR. First, the water in contact with the fuel rods does not boil; only water in the secondary loop is allowed to boil, in a steam generator tank. This allows greater control over the fission process. Second, in a PWR only the water in the primary loop is exposed to radioactivity; the contaminated water never comes in contact with the water in the other loops and never reaches the turbine. In a PWR the residual steam that drives the turbine passes through a condenser, which converts it to water again. The water is then pumped back through two sets of feedwater heaters and pumps. From there it is passed to the steam generator once more.

A vital component of all nuclear reactors is the means to keep the fuel rods from overheating and melting from

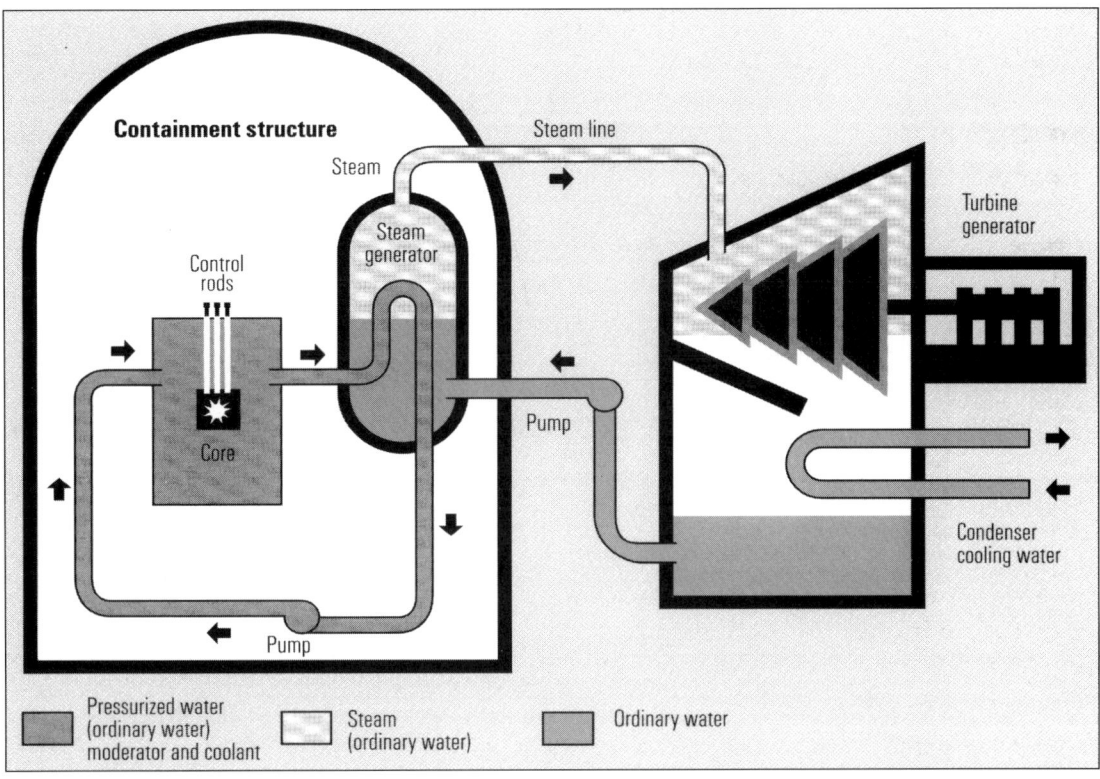

the intense heat of fission. The large cooling towers one sees rising above many nuclear power plants are among the many ways in which the reactor core is kept at a safe temperature. A cooling tower's function is to remove heat from the water that comes out of the condenser. The water is then either discharged into a lake or river or recirculated through the system. (Today, U.S. nuclear power plants operate under regulations that restrict the amount of heated water that can be discharged into bodies of water, so that spawning fish and other wildlife are not affected.)

With an output of just 20 MW of thermal energy and only 5 MW of electric, the Vallecitos reactor generated only one-tenth of the power produced by the Shippingport reactor—but in some ways it was technologically more advanced. Vallecitos was designed to operate either

The pressurized water reactor (PWR) has a number of advantages. First, the water in contact with the fuel rods does not boil; only water in the secondary loop boils. This allows greater control over the fission process. Second, in a PWR only the water in the primary loop is exposed to radioactivity.

by direct transfer of reactor heat from steam to the turbine or via a secondary system that included a steam generator. It was also able to run on both forced and natural circulation of water. Based on its success, the Chicago-based Commonwealth Edison Company signed a contract with GE for the Dresden-1 nuclear power plant in Morris, Illinois. In July 1960, Dresden-1 began operation as the first full-scale commercial nuclear power plant in the United States.

By the 1960s, Westinghouse and GE had gained valuable experience in nuclear power generation. The rivalry between the two companies to convince utility companies of the safety, reliability, and cost-effectiveness of nuclear energy fueled even more rapid development. In 1963, GE launched an aggressive campaign to increase sales of nuclear reactors by offering a so-called turnkey contract to Jersey Central Power and Light Company in New Jersey. GE's proposal was simple but unprecedented: for a fixed sum, it would build the entire plant and then turn it over to the utility. (Turnkey implied that all the utility company need do was turn a key in the door to begin operations.) Most significantly, GE's bid—$66 million—was well below the actual cost of building the new plant. GE officials hoped that the loss would be offset by a resulting upswing in the market for nuclear power. The utility agreed to the terms, and the 515-MW plant went up at Oyster Creek near Toms River, New Jersey. Before long, Westinghouse was also offering turnkey agreements. Both companies suffered millions of dollars in losses to support these arrangements, but the gamble worked: the market for nuclear energy soared. "In 1965, the year before the reactor boom gathered momentum, nuclear vendors sold four nuclear plants with a total of 17 percent of the capacity that utilities purchased that year," according to the NRC. "In 1966, by contrast, utilities bought 20 nuclear units that made up 36 percent of the electrical capacity committed. The following year nuclear vendors sold 31 units that represented 49 percent of the capacity ordered."

Another reason for the boom in nuclear plant construction during the 1960s was the growing public concern with environmental pollution, particularly the pollution caused by power plants that ran on fossil fuels. Public opinion shifted toward nuclear energy as a clean alternative to these fuels. Suddenly, the AEC was flooded with license applications for nuclear power plants—but it had not yet developed standardized criteria for judging the safety and effectiveness of the designs. Under keen pressure by utilities and the public, the AEC struggled to stay abreast of new design developments and rushed to eliminate the backlog of applications, in many cases making what seemed to be arbitrary safety decisions.

The AEC's first major debate over safety regulations focused on the locations of the new plants. The proposed plants were sited within 25 miles of major metropolitan areas. Until the 1960s, the unknown effects of radiation contamination and the uncalculated risk of an accident ensured that nuclear power reactors were sited in isolated or sparsely populated locations. As the industry grew, however, placing the plants in heavily populated areas where electricity was most needed came to be viewed almost as a necessity. The AEC was forced to establish regulations that would allow utilities to build nuclear power plants closer to cities without placing large populations at risk.

Another factor in the nuclear energy explosion concerned the growing practice of power-pooling, in which utilities sold excess power to other companies. This encouraged the construction of larger plants. Even though the fledgling nuclear industry had only successfully operated reactors producing about 200 MW (such as at Shippingport), it followed the lead of the fossil-fuel industry, which regularly expanded by following the "design by extrapolation" concept. The thinking was that what worked for a 200-MW plant would also work for one that produced 500 MW or 1,000 MW, simply by enlarging and expanding the same design.

The next major debate within the AEC focused on containing nuclear reactors in the event of a severe accident. Despite multiple small-scale experiments conducted throughout the 1950s and early 1960s, it was impossible to know for certain what would occur. The concerns became especially worrisome after nuclear power plants increased in size and electrical output—and most of the larger plants did not include stronger or bigger containment buildings in proportion to the larger reactor size. Most experts were confident that the redundant safety features built into the plants would protect the public should a simple accident occur, but they were not so sure what might result when an unexpected chain of events took place.

The greatest fear was of a loss-of-coolant accident (LOCA) in which coolant to the core is lost (by a break in a pipe, for example). The immense heat generated by fission might cause the reactor's fuel rods to melt, and the molten core could feasibly drop to the floor of the containment building and breach the building's integrity. Once the core came in contact with water, a massive steam explosion might result, or radioactive elements might cause a chemical explosion. The scenario that the core could continue melting through the earth was dubbed the "China syndrome," after the fabled belief that China is directly on the other side of the globe from America.

These fears led the ACRS and AEC to focus on the emergency core cooling system (ECCS) of a nuclear reactor—the system that feeds water to the core and maintains its temperature. In 1966 the AEC convened a task force of nuclear specialists to study the problem. The task force's report, published the following year, reiterated that a core meltdown was highly unlikely and that ECCSs were reliable—but it also admitted that in a LOCA, the containment building could be breached. According to the NRC:

> [The report's findings] represented a milestone in the evolution of reactor regulation. . . . Previously, the AEC had viewed the containment building as the final independent line of defense against the release of radiation; even if a serious accident took place the damage it caused would be restricted to the plant. Once it became apparent that under some circumstances the containment building might not hold, however, the key to protecting the public from a large release of radiation was to prevent accidents severe enough to threaten containment. And this depended heavily on a properly designed and functioning ECCS.

An experimental reactor designed to test just such an event—called the Loss-of-Fluids-Test (LOFT) facility—had been in the works at the government's Idaho lab since the beginning of the decade, but the AEC had reduced funding for the project to focus on developing fast-breeder reactors. When LOFT experiments finally took place in the early 1970s, the results were disturbing. Semiscale tests (on much smaller test cores) showed that the ECCS did not function as it was designed. Instead, the superheated, high-pressure steam that built up in the core after the coolant was deliberately removed blocked ECCS water, causing it simply to flow out of the vessel without ever reaching the core.

The findings came at an inopportune time for the AEC, which was struggling under intense pressure from utility companies to streamline power plant licensing. Political support for breeder-reactor research was growing, and the AEC feared losing the support of the president should he learn about the test results. Rather than halt the building of all nuclear reactors, however, the AEC settled on establishing interim safety criteria. These criteria were broadly criticized as too lax, especially in light of the semiscale tests. The contradictory goals of the AEC had come back to haunt its members.

In public hearings about the ECCS tests, the AEC encountered fierce opposition to the construction of new nuclear power plants. Leading AEC officials were replaced, and in 1974, Congress passed the Energy Reorganization Act. The act split the AEC into two new organizations: the NRC, which assumed the AEC's licensing responsibilities, and the Energy Research and Development Agency (later the U.S. Department of Energy), which assumed the role of encouraging nuclear development.

In 1975, the NRC released the results of a study (commissioned by the AEC in 1972) on the safety of nuclear reactors. The report, called WASH-1400 or the Rasmussen Report (after Dr. Norman Rasmussen of the Massachusetts Institute of Technology, who led the study), calculated the probability of a severe nuclear accident occurring in the United States. The report determined that although the risk of a nuclear meltdown was real, it was also highly unlikely—the chance was one in 10,000—and it was a minor risk when compared to the possible occurrence of hurricanes, chemical spills, earthquakes, and airplane accidents.

The report received wide criticism, even from officials

in the NRC. Part of the problem with WASH-1400 was that it relied upon probability statistics, called event trees, that did not consider the fact that several events leading to an accident could be caused by the same mistake. For example, the report estimated that the odds of just one of the auxiliary feedwater valves being closed was one in 1,000. The odds that both valves would be closed at one time was one-thousandth of that, or a million to one.

In January 1979, having studied both the WASH-1400 report and the arguments against it, the NRC withdrew its endorsement of the report. On March 26, 1979—two days before the TMI accident—a plant worker closed both of TMI-2's auxiliary feedwater valves at once. After the accident it was also discovered that workers at the plant never closed one of the valves without also closing the other.

On the morning of the TMI accident, plant operators believed that TMI-2's generators had malfunctioned, a common event. They had no idea that they were in the beginning stages of a major catastrophe.

Thirty Minutes to Meltdown

The accident at TMI-2 was less than a minute old when the safety valves slammed closed and the turbine tripped. Operators believed it was a malfunction of the generators, a relatively common event, and they began the appropriate emergency procedures. Then the reactor scrammed, and they were forced to initiate a more serious emergency plan. Following procedure, shift supervisor Bill Zewe used the plant's public address system to inform workers of the incident. "Unit Two, turbine trip, reactor trip," he announced.

Because a nuclear reactor vessel must be tightly sealed to prevent radiation leakage, it's impossible to see firsthand what's going on inside it. Operators must rely on an elaborate panel of instruments that monitor temperature, pressure, and activity. The first item on the emergency checklist now was to verify that the control rods had correctly dropped into the core during the scram. The instruments told them that they had. Next, operators Craig Faust and Ed Frederick had to determine whether the main feedwater pumps had shut down and the emergency feedwater pumps had turned on. The control panel told Faust that the backup pumps had indeed turned on and were running at full speed.

What Faust did not know was that two days before, during routine testing, a maintenance worker had shut off the backup feedwater flow by closing the pumps' block valves—also called the twelves because they were numbered 12A and 12B on the emergency feedwater checklist. He had never reopened them. One of the NRC's strictest requirements was that these valves not be closed without a complete shutdown of the reactor. Indicator lights on the control panel might have alerted control room operators to the problem, but a maintenance tag attached to a nearby switch obscured at least one of the lights. As a result, Faust assumed the twelves were open and the backup pumps were doing their job.

The design flaws of the complex 40-foot-long control panel created other problems that would soon have dire consequences. The indicator light for the Electromatic relief valve (ERV), one of the brightest signals on the panel, did not tell operators what position the valve was actually in, but rather what the valve was supposed to do according to system commands. Since it had been commanded to close, the panel light was not on, and again Faust believed the valve was functioning properly. But in reality it was not. In the containment building, radioactive coolant continued to flow from the reactor up through the pressurizer, out through the stuck ERV, and into the quench tank at 220 gallons per minute.

It would be two hours and 22 minutes before anyone

realized that the ERV was still open. Other lights, such as those that monitored the quench tank's temperature and pressure, might have alerted them to a problem—but these signals were on a section of the U-shaped control panel that was removed from the main console and facing away from operators. Even the audible alarm for the quench tank went unnoticed because it sounded just like several other alarms going off in the control room.

Without the emergency feedwater pumps transferring water, the steam generators began to boil dry. At this point, the ECCS automatically engaged, sending 1,000 gallons of water per minute through two high-pressure injection pumps into the primary cooling system. As Zewe, Faust, and Frederick reviewed the control panel,

Design flaws and maintenance tags obscured important signals on TMI-2's complex 40-foot-long control panel. The electromatic relief valve (ERV) was open for more than two hours before operators realized the mistake.

they saw that the temperature in the reactor seemed to level out as the ECCS switched on. But they also saw that the pressure was quickly rising, and they interpreted these readings as a sign that the system was completely filling with water—an extremely dangerous situation. "[The water level reading] reached about 385 inches, 400 being the limit," Frederick recalled. A reactor that "goes solid," in nuclear power jargon, is not only very difficult to control, but it can also rupture the pipes in the system and cause radiation leakage. No one was sure precisely how to handle such an event, and fearing that they were facing just that, Frederick reached to his left and pressed six bypass buttons on the control panel. These shut down one of the high-pressure pumps and reduced the flow to 90 gallons per minute in the other.

What had actually happened in TMI-2 was a loss-of-coolant accident—the same problem that had been debated and researched for years by the AEC. It is one of the most potentially serious events that can occur at a nuclear power plant. During a LOCA, restoring the flow of water into the primary cooling loop is absolutely essential to prevent the reactor core from overheating and breaching the reactor vessel. What Ed Frederick had done, however, was exactly the opposite: assuming that the reactor was about to go solid, he had cut off nearly all of its remaining water flow.

Why did TMI-2's operators think the reactor was going solid when it was actually losing coolant? An instrument design flaw in the TMI-2 control panel showed Frederick and his colleagues the coolant level in the pressurizer where the ERV was positioned, not the level of the coolant in the reactor vessel itself. The reactor vessel had by this time become so hot that its coolant was turning to steam, forcing remaining unvaporized coolant up into the pressurizer. This gave control room operators a high reading.

It was now almost 4:07 A.M. If operators had discovered the stuck ERV and had closed it at this point, or if they had allowed the ECCS to continue pumping water, TMI-2 might have been spared. Instead, still fearing that the reactor would go solid, Frederick shut down the second high-pressure pump.

By now, Zewe, Frederick, and Faust, who had been joined by shift foreman Fred Scheimann, were baffled. The control panel appeared to be giving them conflicting information. "We had high temperature and low pressure, and we had a full pressurizer," Frederick remembered. "We were talking about it, trying to figure out what was wrong." As Craig Faust scanned the instrument panel, he noticed what no one had seen before: that the lights alerting them to the closed twelves were on. "The twelves are closed!" he screamed, grabbing the valve controls so quickly that "he nearly ripped them out of the panel," according to Frederick. With water restored to the emergency feedwater pumps, the secondary loop filled with coolant and began drawing heat away from the primary loop again. But one of the two steam generators was now damaged, leaving only one to remove heat from the reactor. And they still hadn't solved the problem inside the reactor itself.

Fourteen minutes into the accident, another alarm went off. The quench tank, filled to bursting, broke a "rupture disk" on its base, spilling one-quarter of a million gallons of steaming radioactive coolant onto the concrete floor of the containment building. When the water level reached two feet, a sump pump engaged and moved the coolant into the auxiliary building that housed the secondary loop, including the turbine, main generator, and main feedwater pump.

The accident was worsening by the second. More than 100 alarms now lit up the control panel. Operators from

TMI-1, which was down for refueling, came to Unit 2's control room to help. Plant functions that the control panel did not track were monitored by a computer that printed out warnings on an electric typewriter. By the time the overflow coolant began pouring into the auxiliary building, the printed messages were already backing up at the typewriter. A warning about the ERV would not print until three hours later.

At about 4:40, workers in the auxiliary building realized that the primary coolant draining from the reactor into the auxiliary building was radioactive. They stopped the transfer, alerted reactor operators, and quickly vacated and sealed off the auxiliary building. But steam and gas from the 9,500 gallons of water already in the building had already escaped through its ventilation system into the atmosphere. This was the first known release of radioactivity during the TMI accident.

It was almost 5:00—less than an hour after local residents heard the roaring steam release—when the reactor core itself began to boil dry. Even though the scram had stopped the fission process, the core was still experiencing "decay heat" produced by radioactive remnants of fission. The intense heat created pockets of steam in the reactor that lowered the water level. The powerful pumps in the primary cooling system began vibrating violently; they were "cavitating," pumping more steam than water. Zewe and the other operators still believed that the core was covered with water and did not understand what was causing the vibration. Still, they knew that the strain from the shuddering pipes could severely damage the machinery, so at 5:20 they shut down one set of cooling pumps. About 20 minutes later, the other set of pumps shut down automatically. The entire cooling system was now at a near standstill.

Between 5:15 and 6:15 A.M., the reactor core of TMI-2

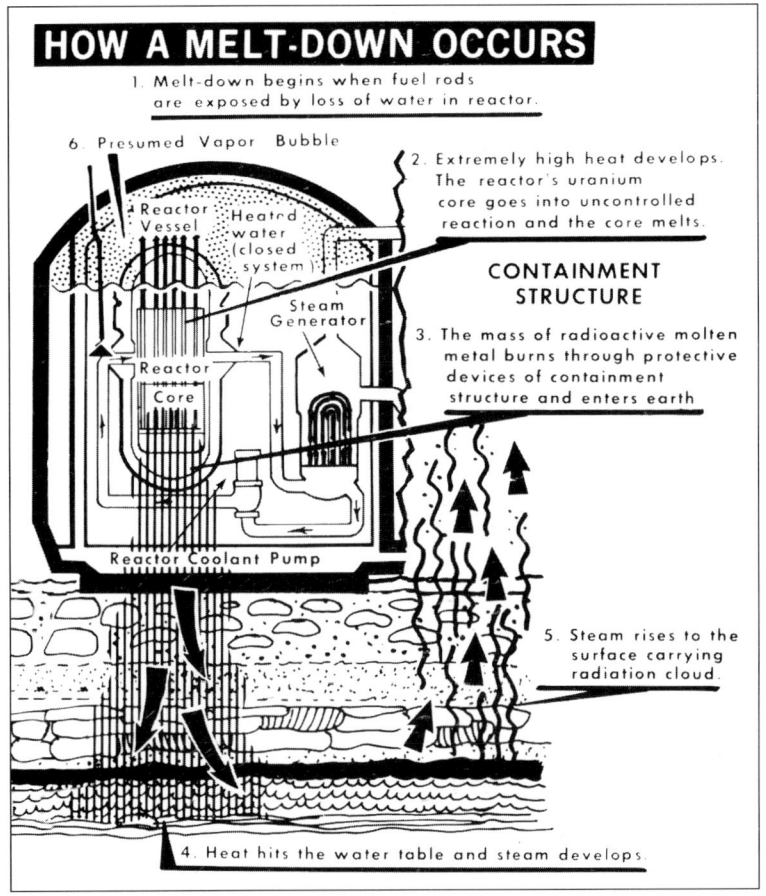

Between 5:15 and 6:15 A.M., the reactor core of TMI-2 began to melt. This diagram shows what would happen in a complete meltdown.

began to melt. The fuel bundles, each about 12 feet long, were more than halfway exposed to air inside the reactor vessel. In the intense heat of the reactor, the zirconium cladding holding the uranium pellets disintegrated, releasing deadly fission products—mostly xenon gas and radioactive iodine—into the primary coolant, which spilled onto the reactor floor. In the concentrated radioactive atmosphere, water molecules split into their components: oxygen, which combined with the disintegrating zirconium, and hydrogen, which rose to the top of the reactor above the exposed fuel rods. The hydrogen and radioactive gases from the coolant escaped through the open ERV and began collecting inside the enormous containment building.

In the control room, operators were having difficulty believing what their instruments were telling them. The computer, overwhelmed by the information it was receiving and unable to process all of it, began printing rows of question marks in place of numbers. Eventually someone contacted Babcock & Wilcox, the builder of the reactor, to see what this meant; they were told only that it signaled a situation the computer was never programmed to deal with. Meanwhile, 24 temperature gauges, called thermocouples, at the top of the reactor building registered 750° F—more than 200° higher than normal.

Because the gauges were designed to measure only the coolant temperature and not that of the core itself, a technician was dispatched to bypass the computer and take readings directly from the thermocouples. The technician was stunned by the results. Every one of the 12 readings measured an astounding 2,000° F or higher. Operators still believed that the core was covered with water, so they could not conceive of it being exposed. They assumed that the thermocouple circuits had malfunctioned.

Zewe and other operators realized that the situation now warranted outside help. By 6:15 they called George Kunder, TMI-2's head of technical support. They had also contacted Gary Miller, the unit's manager; Jack Herbein, Vice President for Electrical Generation at Metropolitan Edison, the company that owned the plant; and Leland Rogers, a representative from Babcock & Wilcox. Only then did they determine that the ERV had been open since 4:00. Finally, at 6:22, it was inactivated via a nearby blocking valve, a motor-driven device mounted on the pressurizer.

But it was too late. Even if the reactor core, which was now two-thirds exposed, could have been cooled by the superheated steam building up in the containment building, the loose pellets of uranium had begun to collapse inward at the core center, forming a solid "cap" that prevented coolant from circulating and created even more concentrated heat. Operators thought that even with the coolant pumps shut down, the core could be cooled by "natural circulation" of water through the pipes in the primary loop—but they didn't know about the steam pockets that were blocking many of the pipes.

At 6:35, an alarm signaling high levels of gamma radiation in the reactor core went off in the control room, but operators never noticed it in the barrage of bells and flashing lights. The typewriter printing alarm status messages was now so far behind that an operator activated a "dump" process in the computer and eliminated about 75 minutes' worth of data in an effort to bring it up to speed. The dumped data was unretrievable.

A few minutes later, technicians took a coolant sample from a drain line between the containment building and the auxiliary building. The sample was extremely "hot"—350 times more radioactive than normal. A worker sent into the auxiliary building with a handheld radiation monitor returned with a similarly dire reading: a radiation level of 1,000 millirems, thousands of times higher than the acceptable "background" (naturally occurring) level.

With radiation levels soaring outside the containment building, TMI-2 operators sprang into action. "Just about 6:50," Bill Zewe remembers, "all of these alarms started . . . going amber-red, amber-red on all indicators [amber signals an alert; red signals an alarm], and I knew that we had a tremendous problem." At 6:56 A.M., Zewe set off a siren and declared a site emergency over the plant's public address system.

A site emergency is declared at a nuclear power plant when an incident threatens an uncontrolled release of radioactivity into the immediate area of the plant. This requires that certain critical areas of the plant be evacuated and that plant managers notify local authorities. Bill Zewe ordered his workers to alert Pennsylvania Emergency Management Agency (PEMA) and the civil defense department of Dauphin County, where TMI is located. But all of the operators, including those who began coming in to start their shifts that morning, were still misreading the many indications that a LOCA was in progress. They could not determine why the control panel showed contradictory information. Meanwhile, technicians began the process of trying to measure exactly how much radiation may have escaped from the reactor.

The standard unit of measurement for a radiation dose is a millirem, or one-thousandth of a rem. You might absorb one millirem of radiation from a year of watching TV or of wearing a wristwatch with a luminous dial. Normal levels near the plant were about 100 millirems per year. The average American is exposed to about 200 millirems per year, including doses from medical procedures such as X rays. TMI employees wore indicator badges that measured their exposure levels; plant workers could receive no more than 5 rems per year of radiation. At 7:24, station manager Gary Miller received an unbelievable reading from a monitor on the containment building dome. The monitor showed that radiation from the damaged fuel was "shining"—penetrating the thick steel walls of the reactor vessel—at 8 rems per hour. When the shielding near the detector was taken into account, this actually corresponded to 800 rems per hour. Accounting for the shielding properties of the vessel, experts from Pennsylvania's Bureau of Radiological Protection (BRP) calculated that residents directly west of the plant, on the shore of the Susquehanna River, were possibly being exposed to 10 rems per hour.

Suddenly, the gravity of the accident became very

1. A Cooling Malfunction Caused Pressure In Nuclear Reactor Which Was Then Automatically Shut Down.

2. Reactor Coolant Water Floods Reactor Building Basement; Is Pumped To Auxiliary Building Where It Floods Again.

3. Radioactive Gases Released Into Atmosphere In Two Ways:
   1. In Deliberate Cooling Process Wednesday, Company Released Radioactive Steam Through Stack.
   2. Additional Radioactive Vapor From Spilled Water Has Been Leaking Out Of Auxiliary Building Since Accident.

4. On Friday, New Radioactive Gases Were Released To Reduce Pressure In The Reactor As The Company Struggled With Unexpected Delay In Coolant Process.

Radiation levels both inside and outside the containment building soared during the first hours of the accident. A general emergency was declared on Wednesday, March 28. This graphic outlines some of the events of the disaster.

clear. Miller changed the status of the accident from a site emergency to a general emergency. In the history of the commercial nuclear power industry, no one had ever declared a general emergency. Officially, this meant that the accident occurring at TMI-2 posed a serious threat of radiation release that could affect the general public, not just the immediate plant vicinity.

Clarence Deller was on duty in PEMA's concrete underground bunker beneath the State Transportation Building in Harrisburg, 10 miles from TMI, when he received a call from TMI-2's operators. The message notified him of a site emergency, and the caller requested that Deller contact the BRP. Deller posted an alert on the teletype machine for civil defense directors of the four surrounding counties. He also alerted local fire and police departments. When he couldn't reach anyone at the BRP office, he called William Dornsife, a nuclear engineer and the duty officer, at his home. "I rolled out of bed when the phone rang. . . . I was hoping against hope that this was a drill," Dornsife said later. By the time Dornsife phoned TMI-2, however, the situation had worsened. "There was an announcement in the background to evacuate the fuel handling auxiliary building. It didn't hit me until I heard that." When Dornsife heard about the radiation measurements from the containment building dome, he realized that some of the fuel in the reactor must have melted. He immediately called his radiation monitoring team.

The operators at TMI-2 were also required to inform the NRC's regional office, located near Philadelphia in King of Prussia, PA. But when they called the NRC office shortly after 7:00 A.M., they reached an answering service. The office did not open until eight o'clock. At the same time, PEMA director and retired Army colonel Oren K. Henderson was calling Governor Dick Thornburgh. By the time TMI-2 finally established communication with the NRC and Thornburgh was advised of the accident, a vent gas monitor on Unit 2 had registered radiation releases more than 100 times higher than normal. "The minute I heard that there had been an accident at a nuclear facility," Thornburgh recalls, "I knew we were in another dimension."

Around that time, Dave Edwards, a traffic reporter for Harrisburg's Top 40 radio station WKBO, was driving through the state capital on his morning sweep of the city. Over his car's CB radio he received a call from a friend who'd heard that a local fire company had been put on alert because of problems at TMI. Edwards called Mike Pintek, WKBO's news director. Pintek hadn't heard anything, so he contacted County Control, who fielded most of the fire and police calls for Dauphin County. When that office didn't have any information,

Pintek tried to contact Jack Herbein, whose business card he'd picked up during a recent press tour of the Three Mile Island facility.

The flustered switchboard operator at TMI put Pintek through to the control room of Unit 2 instead. The news director heard utter confusion on the line. "I can't talk now, we've got a problem," said the technician who answered. "Call Reading [PA] and talk to them." The headquarters of Metropolitan Edison (Met Ed), the utility company that owned the plant, were in Reading, PA, about 35 miles from Three Mile Island. Pintek finally managed to get through to Blain Fabian, Met Ed's chief public relations officer, who confirmed that a general emergency had been declared. Fabian assured Pintek that it was a formality required by the NRC. Pintek asked whether that meant there was any danger to the general public. Fabian said no.

At 8:25, WKBO went on the air with a five-minute news update that included the announcement of a general emergency at TMI and reassurances that the plant's owners saw no danger to the public. It was the first news broadcast of the problem, and the world's first hint that one of the worst nuclear accidents in history had begun.

Guards restrict access to the island during the TMI crisis. The workers dressed in radiation suits were in the area of the building where the accident occurred.

"An Incident of Some Moment"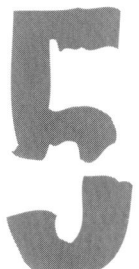

The call that TMI-2 operators made to the NRC triggered a series of procedures required by the federal government during a nuclear emergency. The King of Prussia regional NRC office contacted NRC national headquarters in Bethesda, Maryland, and established a direct phone line to the TMI-2 control room. In Bethesda, NRC decision-makers opened the Incident Response Center (IRC), a suite of conference rooms and offices outfitted with computers and other communication equipment to keep the agency informed during an emergency. At 8:45 A.M., a team of inspectors from the King of Prussia office sped 86 miles westward on the Pennsylvania Turnpike, van lights flashing, so the inspectors could assess the situation in person.

As the IRC began filling with industry and government specialists, a long list of federal agencies was also notified, including the Department of Energy; the Environmental Protection, Federal Preparedness, and Defense Civil Preparedness Agencies; the Department of Health, Education, and Welfare; and the Federal Disaster Assistance Administration. More than 20 telephone lines in the IRC connected specialists with nuclear experts around the country.

At about 9:00, National Security Council staff member Jessica Matthews, the council's expert on nuclear issues in Washington, received two urgent calls. The first was from NRC Commissioner Victor Gilinsky, informing her that an "incident of some moment" had occurred at Three Mile Island. The other call came from the situation room in the White House itself: at least two of the federal agencies that were notified about TMI apparently had the same thoughts as Gilinsky. Matthews quickly drafted a memo outlining the information she'd received and sent it to National Security Advisor Zbigniew Brzezinski, who immediately briefed President Jimmy Carter. It was now 10:00 A.M. Matthews recalled that even though her facts were incomplete, the situation at TMI didn't sound threatening. "It looked like things were under control," she later told the *Washington Post*.

In Dauphin County, Pennsylvania, however, the crisis was more immediate and unsettling. Earlier that morning, county civil defense director Kevin Molloy had received PEMA official Clarence Deller's alert about the accident and rushed to his office in Harrisburg to help contact other civil defense officials, local mayors, police and fire units, and state authorities. Molloy's job was not to learn the technical details of the accident but to determine how to protect the public. He was already thinking about radiation danger. "My first reaction was: Do we have to evacuate?" he recalled. But accurate information about what was really happening at TMI-2 was increasingly hard to come by. Initial reports warned of a site emergency; but as Molloy arrived in his office he received a second call: a general emergency had been declared. No one seemed to know what the difference was or what the status change meant in terms of public health and safety. PEMA director Oren Henderson later admitted, "We lacked so much knowledge about what was going on [at TMI]."

The lack of solid information was at best frustrating; at worst it was infuriating, recalls Robert Reid, high school instructor and mayor of Middletown, three miles from the power plant:

> I was notified of the accident at 8:45 A.M. . . . from that time until 11:00 A.M. we didn't know what was going on. The information that we were getting was . . . being given out on TV. And as we changed from channel to channel, we got different information. At 11:00 I decided to call down to the Island. They . . . told me to call Met Ed's office in Reading. . . . The man I was supposed to talk to was in a meeting and I was told he'd call me back. . . . [A]nother man did, and he said, "Mayor, I want to assure you that no radioactive particles escaped and no one was injured." I said, "Well, that's great!" I went out to my car, turned on the radio, and there it was as big as you please: the announcer . . . [was] saying there were radioactive particles that had escaped. . . . I didn't know what to believe. And it went that way the entire day.

Goldsboro mayor Ken Meyers had a similar experience. "I got a phone call from my mother at work at

10:00 on Wednesday [March 28th]; that's how I found out," he said in an interview two months later. When Meyers learned about a possible radiation leak at TMI, he thought it odd that an emergency vehicle had driven through the streets of Goldsboro asking residents to stay inside with doors and windows closed. "What [went] through my mind [was] this: I don't think shutting the doors and windows will keep it out," Meyers remembered.

The third and last call Kevin Molloy received from TMI did little to clarify the situation. A radiological officer explained that the core was covered but that they were getting high radiation readings. The readings could be "erroneous," the man continued, "but we can't rely on that." Molloy waited for further instructions from TMI or the state government, but heard nothing. The officer was wrong—by the time he spoke with Molloy, the fuel rods in the reactor core were two-thirds exposed and were beginning to melt.

Wire services across the country picked up the TMI story after WKBO broke the news. The *New York Times, Los Angeles Times, Washington Post,* CBS, NBC, ABC, the British Broadcasting Company (BBC), and scores of other news organizations around the world dispatched reporters and photographers to the Harrisburg area to cover what still appeared to be a minor accident. Because the gravity of what was happening was not yet clear—and because nuclear energy issues were commonly deemed too complex or too boring for most people—almost none of the original news reporters on the scene were science specialists. Most were simply those who arrived at work earliest that morning or who happened to be in or near Pennsylvania on other assignments. As a result, many of the first reports to reach the public were not

only incomplete but were also wildly inaccurate. Reporters had had no better luck in reaching plant or company spokespeople than had local emergency workers and officials.

The power plant's owner, Met Ed, did little to clarify the stream of misinformation pouring out of TMI-2. It had first heard about the accident some time after 7 A.M., when a plant official called Reading-based engineer Richard Klingaman. Klingaman

Wire services across the country picked up the TMI story after local radio station WKBO broke the news. Reporters and photographers from around the world gathered at the gates of TMI to cover what at first appeared to be a minor accident.

reported the accident to George Troffer, of Met Ed's quality assurance department, who notified Robert Arnold, a vice president of parent company General Public Utilities (GPU). Arnold dictated a press statement, but it mentioned no off-site release of radiation from TMI; nor did it reveal that a general emergency was in progress. In fact, the statement contained so much technical information that many members of the communications staff at Met Ed did not bother to read it to callers. "I didn't understand it," said one staff member, "[and] I didn't feel I could explain it to anyone."

Meanwhile, TMI-2 shift supervisor Bill Zewe had already contacted Met Ed's vice president of electrical generation, Jack Herbein, who with chief public relations officer Blain Fabian drew up another official statement. "The nuclear reactor at Three Mile Island Unit 2 was shut down as prescribed when a malfunction related to a feedwater pump occurred about four A.M. Wednesday," it read. "The entire unit . . . will be out of service for about a week while equipment is checked and repairs made." Fabian, who had told WKBO's Mike Pintek that all was well, knew that this upbeat assessment was inaccurate, but he was reluctant to release news of a serious accident until it had been confirmed by TMI-2 station manager Gary Miller. Until that happened, all that the outside world knew about the accident was contained in the official statement.

Bill Gross, the supervisor of the Met Ed observation center across the river from Three Mile Island, was stunned when he arrived at work at 7:00 A.M. to face hundreds of employees and reporters milling about on the lawn and inside the building. Gross, who had no idea what had happened, was welcomed with a barrage of questions. Not until 9:30 was he able to speak with Gary Miller and formulate a third official Met Ed statement, which he read at 10:00. The plant, Gross announced, was being brought to an "orderly cold shutdown" after "radioactive cold water was released inside the reactor building." Plant officials were checking for radiation releases but hadn't found any, "and we do not expect any."

Again, this was not the complete story, or even an accurate report of what was happening inside TMI-2. Operators had already learned that radiation was passing through the reactor vessel at eight rems per hour and may have been exposing the population of Goldsboro, west and downwind of the plant, to radiation levels hundreds of times higher than normal. Still, when the BRP sent a helicopter team over Goldsboro to monitor radiation levels, they returned with encouraging results: no significant radiation was detected.

As Bill Gross read his statement, the NRC officials from King of Prussia arrived at Three Mile Island. On the way to Unit 2, they saw workers roping off areas that were "hot," or contaminated with radiation. In one hot zone they spotted a makeshift sign that read, "DON'T WALK. RUN!" The scene was eerie. "As we were walking through the turbine building, which was basically like a ghost town . . . we saw these two other people from the plant wearing their anti-contamination radiation suits, and they also had their respirator masks on," recalls Jim Higgins, one of the NRC experts. "[T]his is an area of the plant that normally is not contaminated. . . . And it gave the impression [that there was] something very wrong here." As the NRC scientists reached the control room, Gary Miller was sending some workers out of

At TMI-2 operators measured the radiation passing through the reactor vessel at eight rems per hour. The reactor may have been exposing the population of Goldsboro, west and downwind of the plant, to radiation levels hundreds of times higher than normal.

the building. Xenon gas that had vented into the air was now seeping into the control room as the wind changed direction, requiring operators to wear respirator masks—and there were not enough of them to protect all the workers.

Although necessary, the helmet-like masks made it difficult for operators to communicate and nearly impossible to speak on the telephone. By then, those in the plant were so desperate for information on how to solve the increasingly dire problem in the reactor vessel that at times they disregarded the safety regulations. "I know there were a couple of times when I just took my respirator off and talked real quickly in the phone and put it back on and said, 'Okay, well, let's do it as quickly as I can,'" Higgins admits, "but we—we just had to try to get the information through."

Worse yet, only two phone lines ran directly into Unit 2, and they were continually tied up. Babcock & Wilcox, the Virginia-based designers of the TMI-2 reactor, tried for five hours to get through to the control room. Even the NRC's incident response center could not establish a direct line and was forced to follow a circuitous route to get information to and from Unit 2. Mike Gray was a trained engineer and the writer of the screenplay for the eerily prophetic film *The China Syndrome,* which had premiered just 12 days before the accident. Gray heard about the situation and flew from Los Angeles, California, to offer technical assistance and report on the incident. He recalls:

> [T]hey had to relay all the information through a regional NRC office in King of Prussia, Pennsylvania, to the Unit 1, which is north of the accident, and then a runner would run over to Unit 2 and read the [radiation] gauge and run back and report this. So . . . people . . . are getting fourth-hand information which is largely incorrect, and certainly incomplete, and they're passing back advice which doesn't make it all the way [to the proper officials].

At noon, eight hours after the first sign of trouble at TMI-2, Jim Higgins and NRC investigator Charles Gallina finally established a dedicated phone line from Unit 2 to the IRC in Bethesda.

In the meantime, the reactor's core was still uncovered and temperature and radiation readings continued to rise. From 800 rems per hour at 7:24 A.M. —the level that triggered a general emergency— radiation in the containment dome had soared to a staggering 40,000 to 50,000 rems per hour by 10:30. Gary Miller now realized that steam pockets had probably formed in the pipes and were preventing primary coolant from circulating. But he also believed that the core was covered and still feared the reactor might go solid. Rather than reactivate the cooling pumps, he decided to open the motorized blocking valve on the pressurizer—the same one that had closed off the malfunctioning ERV earlier. This would force the system pressure to drop to 500 pounds per square inch, at which point it would trigger an automatic core-flooding process, pumping 500,000 gallons of coolant into the reactor and lowering the core temperature.

When control room operators opened the blocking valve, the system pressure began to decrease. Within hours it dropped from more than 1,000 pounds per square inch to 600—but it never reached the trigger point for the core flooding to occur. Without realizing it, Miller had made the situation worse. Rather than being reimmersed in coolant, the reactor core started losing even more coolant through the opened block valve. As the fuel rods continued to decay, a chemical reaction between the zirconium cladding and the radioactive water produced hydrogen, which rose to the top of the reactor vessel in a vast "bubble." Some of the hydrogen escaped through the block valve and collected in the containment building itself.

Around 2:00 P.M., as TMI-2 operators struggled to control the pressure in the containment building,

Miller heard what sounded like a valve slamming in the reactor building. At the same moment, Ed Frederick saw the containment pressure gauge needle leap from two to 28 pounds per square inch. With the spike, another protective process engaged: a series of spray valves inside the building began to douse the decaying materials with sodium hydroxide to prevent shining. But the chemical spray would virtually destroy the machinery, so Ed Frederick deactivated it.

Not until days later would anyone realize that what Miller and Frederick had heard and monitored on the gauge was a hydrogen explosion powerful enough to destroy a building. Only the thick concrete walls of the containment structure prevented a catastrophe.

Outside Three Mile Island, confusion reigned. At 11:00 in Harrisburg, a routine press conference on energy policy turned into a briefing on the developing situation at TMI. Lieutenant Governor Bill Scranton had delayed the conference while he gathered more information from Met Ed. Although the thirtyish lieutenant governor was the youngest in state history, he was well-versed in nuclear power issues, serving also as chairman of the state Civil Defense and Energy Councils. "Everything is under control," he assured the press. "There is and was no danger to public health and safety. . . . No increase in normal radiation levels has been detected." As Scranton fielded questions, however, he was interrupted by nuclear engineer William Dornsife, who just learned from plant officials that there had, in fact, been a "small amount" of radioactive material detected in the ground off-site.

Having just heard about the release of radiation, Scranton was startled and angered to discover minutes after his press conference that Met Ed was still declaring the opposite. "The indignation that welled up within me was memorable," Scranton says. "I still haven't gotten over that. It was at that point that I realized that we could not rely on Metropolitan Edison for the kind of information we needed to make decisions." At 4:30 P.M., following a confrontational meeting with Met Ed's Jack Herbein, Scranton called a second press conference. "This situation is more complex than the company first led us to believe," he announced bluntly. "Metropolitan Edison has given you and us conflicting information. . . . There has been a release of radioactivity into the environment." He reassured reporters that so far no danger to the public health existed. By now, most members of the press had researched the subject and were asking better-informed questions. For the first time, the press learned that fuel rod damage had occurred in the reactor. It was now clear that this was no minor accident.

At Babcock & Wilcox in Virginia, one of TMI's most experienced operators, Jim Floyd, was taking a refresher course on the TMI reactors. Company officials realized that he was in the building and sent for him at once. According to author Mike Gray, Floyd's response was immediate: "Turn on the emergency core cooling system, whatever else is going on. Open those pumps. Get high pressure injection started. Keep flow at 400 gallons a minute or else."

About an hour after Scranton's second press conference, TMI-2 operators restarted the ECCS, following Floyd's urgent instructions. As primary coolant began to recirculate, the exposed and decaying top of the core was finally submerged again. The temperature inside the reactor dropped and pressure stabilized. By Wednesday night, it appeared that

"AN INCIDENT OF SOME MOMENT"   67

Lieutenant Governor Bill Scranton realized that Met Ed was not providing reliable information. He called a press conference and stated, "Metropolitan Edison has given you and us conflicting information. . . . There has been a release of radioactivity into the environment."

the worst was over. CBS *Evening News* anchor Walter Cronkite opened his program that evening with a fairly optimistic report on TMI: "It was the first step in a nuclear nightmare—[and] as far as we know at this hour, no worse than that."

On Thursday, March 29, Met Ed launched a campaign to convince the public that the crisis had indeed passed. On ABC's *Good Morning, America,* company president Walter Creitz assured viewers that Unit 2 would soon be closed down and that all was well. Later that morning, however, the official company composure seemed to crack. When Creitz introduced Jack Herbein at a press conference in Hershey, Pennsylvania, 120 reporters who had endured gruff and tight-lipped treatment from the vice president on Wednesday now gave him no quarter. One of them questioned the accuracy of Herbein's report on the core temperature; another insisted on knowing whether there was actual core damage. Middletown mayor Robert Reid demanded to know why the company had waited three hours to warn local residents about the accident. Herbein denied withholding information. Finally, he lost his temper. "We didn't injure anybody with this accident; we didn't seriously contaminate anybody, and we certainly didn't kill anybody," he snapped.

Unable to get reliable information from Met Ed, the governor's office turned to the NRC. In a third state press conference on Wednesday, NRC officials in Harrisburg reported that although equipment failures and radiation leakage had occurred, TMI-2's situation was manageable. But even after Jim Higgins and Charles Gallina briefed the governor and his staff, confusion remained over the real level of radiation danger.

On Thursday afternoon, a U.S. Congressional delegation arrived in Pennsylvania for a firsthand assessment of TMI-2. Along with Congressman John Wydler of New York, Lieutenant Governor Bill Scranton was fitted with an anticontamination radiation suit and permitted to enter the unit's auxiliary building. "It occurred to me, 'Someone's got to go down there and look at that place,'"

At a press conference, Met Ed's Jack Herbein (left) denied withholding information and lost his temper. "We didn't injure anybody with this accident; we didn't seriously contaminate anybody, and we certainly didn't kill anybody," he snapped.

Scranton said in 1999. "I being, you know, 30 years old and maybe thinking I was more immortal than I really was, said, 'I'm going to go down there.'" Scranton remembers feeling as though he were preparing to "go on a space walk":

> It took me 45 minutes to get in all of the suits and putting all of the dosimeters on me [devices for measuring personal exposure to radiation] . . . and the

protective boots and everything. . . . And I must say I was quite unnerved the closer I got to it.

When I started walking in . . . I saw on the floor this water, which looked like . . . water in your basement except it happened to be in the auxiliary building of a nuclear power plant. I realized that what was around me was highly contaminated. But I came back with a much clearer understanding of what was going on that island.

Scranton later reported that the dosimeters revealed he had been exposed to 80 millirems of radiation. "And I feel fine," he added.

Not everyone was convinced that the danger was past. NRC officials in Bethesda were alarmed by the reactor's slow recovery, but without a sample of the primary coolant from the reactor, no one knew for sure how bad the situation was. While Met Ed was holding the Hershey press conference, antinuclear activists Dr. Ernest Sternglass, a radiology professor at the University of Pittsburgh, and Dr. George Wald, a Nobel laureate and former Harvard University biologist, convened a press conference of their own in the state capital. "Every dose [of radiation] is an overdose," Sternglass told the reporters. "A little radiation does a little harm; a lot does more harm." Sternglass and Wald emphasized that infants, unborn children, and pregnant women in the vicinity of TMI were at the greatest risk. They revealed that they had conducted their own radiation tests near the Harrisburg airport (three miles north of the plant), and that the levels were 15 times higher than normal.

Fearful of causing a panic, most local radio and TV stations did not report Sternglass and Wald's warnings. WKBO's Mike Pintek decided to go ahead with the story, however. Almost immediately, the radio station, local hospitals, and agencies of the state government were flooded with calls from frightened residents asking what they should do. At 4:00 P.M. on Thursday, Governor Dick Thornburgh called a press conference, intending to allay the growing fears of central Pennsylvanians: "I believe, at this point, that there is no cause for alarm, nor any reason to disrupt your daily routine, nor any reason to feel that public health has been affected by the events on Three Mile Island. I realize that you are being subjected to a conflicting array of information from a wide variety of sources. So am I. I spent virtually the entire last 36 hours trying to separate fact from fiction. . . . I feel that we have succeeded on the more important questions."

On Friday, March 30, however, Governor Thornburgh was forced to take back his assurances.

Early on Friday, March 29, a potentially dangerous buildup of radioactive gas in TMI-2 was vented to the surrounding area. A second site emergency was declared and the NRC recommended evacuation of area residents.

"The World Has Never Known a Day Quite Like Today"

Early on Friday, March 29, shift supervisor Jim Floyd, back from his trip to the Babcock & Wilcox plant, faced a potentially dangerous buildup of radioactive gas in the TMI-2 makeup tank. The tank, part of the ECCS, was meant to hold water for the emergency high-pressure injection system that cooled the reactor core. Floyd had a choice: he could relieve the buildup either by venting the gas into a waste-gas decay tank or into the outside air. Normally it would be logical to vent into the tank, but Floyd knew that this was risky because the transfer line to the tank had leaks. He also feared that the valve on the makeup tank might malfunction and remain open. On the other hand, if he vented outside and the valve stuck, a potentially high level of radioactivity would be released into the surrounding area.

After some thought, Floyd notified PEMA of his decision to vent outside. In the meantime, he sent up a specialist in a helicopter to monitor radiation levels above the plant during the venting. When he opened the valve at about 7:35 A.M., the radiation level rose from a typical three to five millirems per hour to 1,200 millirems, then dropped to normal levels when he closed the valve at about 8:15. As a formality, plant officials declared a site emergency. TMI-2 operators again contacted PEMA to report the results.

With the second call to PEMA, a series of miscommunications was set in motion. NRC public-relations official Karl Abraham passed on the readings from the venting to Harold Denton, head of the NRC's Operating Reactor Division—but Abraham didn't have complete details. He could not say whether the 1,200-millirem level was detected off-site. Denton and other Bethesda IRC officials, already concerned that the waste-gas decay tank might be full (though in reality it was not), assumed that it was an off-site reading and that Abraham's news was proof that their fears had been realized.

Alarmed, the NRC called Governor Thornburgh to report that the radiation level above the plant had soared, and then notified the White House of a possible new hazard in Pennsylvania. "[B]y Friday morning the whole picture was one of uncertainty," Denton recalls. "I sort of saw this puff release of radiation as being the last straw. It kind of destroyed my confidence that we really knew what was going on up there."

Although local officials at the state's BRP knew that the radiation level had dropped immediately and were unconcerned, PEMA director Oran Henderson felt differently. "[T]he way it was related to me," he said later, "I was about ninety percent certain that we were going to execute an evacuation." At 10:00 A.M., Governor Thornburgh made a public announcement urging everyone within 10 miles of

This worker checks for radioactivity in Middletown, PA. TMI's cooling towers are visible in the background.

Three Mile Island to stay indoors until further notice. In communities throughout the region, civil defense workers armed with Geiger counters and dosimeters drove through the streets in vehicles equipped with loudspeakers. They warned people to stay inside with doors and windows closed, check TV and radio reports regularly for further information, and stay off phone lines. School officials kept students indoors during recesses.

At 11:15 A.M., the terrifying sound of air raid sirens erupted in the city of Harrisburg. To this day, no one knows who set off the blast. Some believe that it was a well-meaning civil defense worker who wanted to emphasize the governor's warning. Whatever the intent, the sirens sparked panic in the city and the surrounding area. Even though no official evacuation orders had been issued, news had leaked to the local population about an "uncontrolled" release of radioactivity from TMI-2 that morning.

The panic spread quickly. Matt Magda, who worked for the state's historical and museum commission in Harrisburg, heard the news on the radio at 9:00 and called his wife, Suzanne, a teacher at Bishop McDevitt High School, nine miles from TMI. "I had been suspicious [of TMI] all along and now I was sure something major was going on," Magda said in a 1980 interview. "I told her . . . I would get suitcases together and other items that we would need, and I would assume that she would get [to our house]; if not, she would arrive at the end of the [school] day, and we would take off." Suzanne recalled the frenzy she witnessed as she headed home: "I saw people outside their houses with all their car doors open, just pitching food and clothing and household goods . . . into their cars."

Harold Denton realized he needed to act immediately. If radioactivity really was leaking from TMI-2, the "plume" would not wait for NRC officials to conduct a careful analysis. "The exposure would already be there," he said. He decided to recommend evacuation and gave the go-ahead to Harold Collins of the NRC's office of state programs. But instead of following TMI and Pennsylvania procedures and alerting the BRP, Collins contacted Henderson at PEMA. Henderson in turn called Lieutenant Governor Scranton and Governor Thornburgh, then alerted the Dauphin, Lancaster, York, and Cumberland County civil defense directors. Like the other county officials, Kevin Molloy of the Dauphin County office immediately called fire companies and other emergency workers—but he also decided to warn residents via the radio.

With the radio announcements of evacuations, the growing panic over the accident at TMI became near hysteria. Mark Stephens, who later served on the President's Commission on the Accident at Three Mile Island, describes the reactions of terrified residents:

> Within an hour after Molloy made his announcement, more than 137,000 telephone calls were made in Harrisburg—10 times the normal load and more than two calls for each man, woman and child.... Many people simply got in their cars and left the area.... One woman in York, 12 miles from the plant, withdrew $100,000 in savings bonds from her safe-deposit box, afraid they would be contaminated [with radioactive fallout]. The Federal Reserve sent an additional $7 million in cash to local banks to cover panic withdrawals.
>
> An automobile dealer in Harrisburg sold 21 cars on Friday—the highest one-day sale in his dealership's history. "Nobody even wanted to haggle," he said, "and a couple of them even paid with cash money." ...
>
> Barb Taylor went to help another teacher at Herbert Hoover Elementary School in Harrisburg. When she returned to her fourth-grade classroom, she found the children writing their wills.

At about 11:30, Met Ed's Jack Herbein appeared before hundreds of reporters and cameramen. Transmitted live on five local radio stations, he announced that conditions at TMI-2 were "stable." When questioned, he admitted that the radiation release earlier that morning was a deliberate venting, but insisted that the radiation level of the release was 350 millirems rather than 1,200. As for the evacuation recommendations, Herbein said, "If the civil defense chooses to tell inhabitants of Middletown to keep their windows and doors shut, that's their prerogative. We have our windows and doors open." Why didn't Met Ed notify the public about the release? reporters demanded. "I don't know why we need to . . . tell you each and every thing that we do," replied Herbein.

Furious with what he believed was stonewalling on the part of Met Ed, WKBO news director Mike Pintek exploded. "I remember feeling very angry and I—I shouted a question to Jack Herbein something along the lines of, 'You started to melt that thing down, didn't you? *Didn't you?*' . . . I guess at that moment I was not a journalist any more, I was a—I lived here and I was mad. I was angry." In the uproar, one announcement was almost completely overlooked: Herbein stated that a bubble of hydrogen gas had once again accumulated at the top of the reactor core.

Governor Thornburgh spent Friday morning meeting with PEMA officials, conferring with NRC chairman Joseph Hendrie in Washington, DC, and speaking with President Carter himself. Despite an almost continuous closed-door meeting among NRC commissioners about the mounting problem, no one was certain of the plant's status or whether an immediate danger of radiation overexposure existed. Less than three hours after Thornburgh warned area residents to stay indoors, he made another statement: "I am advising pregnant women and preschool-age children to leave the area within a five-mile radius of the Three Mile Island facility until further notice. We have also ordered the closing of any schools within this area. I repeat that this and other contingency measures are based on my belief that an excess of caution is best. Current readings are no higher than they were yesterday."

"THE WORLD HAS NEVER KNOWN A DAY QUITE LIKE TODAY"

Despite the carefully chosen wording advising residents to evacuate, the governor's announcement touched off a mass exodus. Throughout the afternoon and evening, 40,000 people in the Three Mile Island vicinity left their homes in fear. In the next few days, 100,000 more would follow. Family members who were not in the same place had difficulty reaching others via overloaded phone circuits; in some area buildings the phone lines went dead. Marsha McHenry, a nearby resident, tearfully

Governor Thornburgh's announcement advising pregnant women and young children to evacuate touched off a mass exodus in the area around TMI. Here, nearby Middletown has turned into a ghost town.

remembers what came to be called "Black Friday" by locals: "The moment that's so crystal clear in my mind is driving on the highway and trying to imagine what would happen to this area. All of this beautiful countryside would be destroyed. It would be so contaminated that nobody could be there for hundreds of years. I looked as hard as I could at everything, and tried to burn it into my mind, what everything looked like, because I wasn't going to see it again."

But there was another major problem: of all the communities within a five-mile radius of TMI, not a single one had a viable evacuation plan in place. Five years earlier, when Unit 1 first went on-line, Met Ed had assured locals that the plant was so safe that evacuation plans were unnecessary. Although Dauphin County official Kevin Molloy and Middletown mayor Robert Reid had tried to develop an emergency strategy among fire, police, and civil defense workers in the area, it was difficult to get a consensus. Reid was in the early stages of putting together his own town's plan when news of the accident broke on Wednesday.

Governor Thornburgh, in office just over two months, was stunned when he learned of this state of affairs. He asked a trusted and top-ranking staff member to give him an assessment. "His report . . . was chilling, to say the least," Thornburgh recalled in 1999. "One of the things I'll never forget was that he said that under the regimen that had been established by Dauphin County where Harrisburg was, and Cumberland County, across the river, . . . their evacuees would meet head-on in the middle of the bridge over which they were to be evacuated." Thornburgh and his aides immediately set to work retooling the weak plans should a full evacuation prove necessary.

Because no official evacuation routes had been planned in the event of an accident at TMI, no evacuee

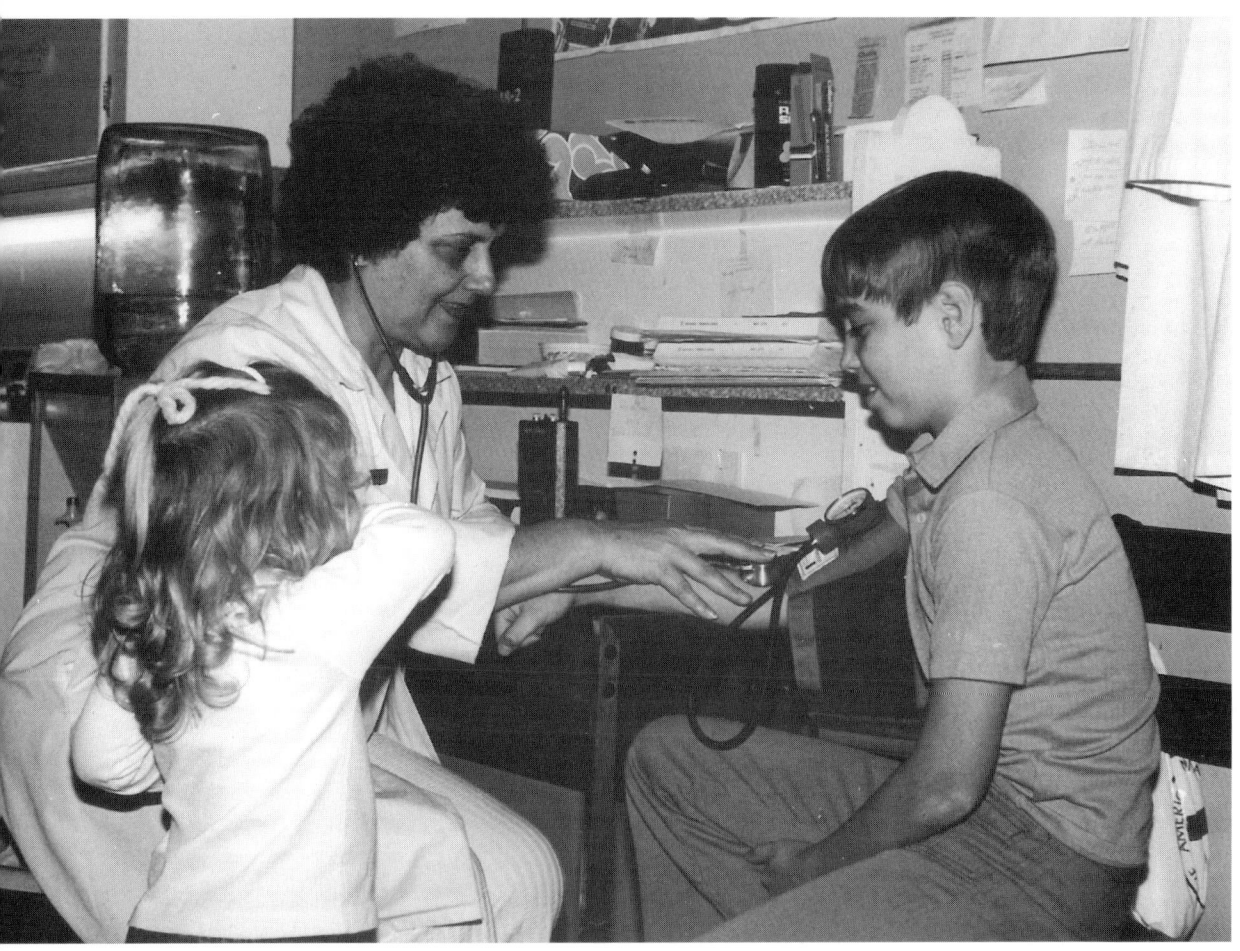

Jean DeAngelis, an occupational health nurse who headed first aid facilities for the Hershey Entertainment and Resorts Company, organized a temporary shelter for TMI evacuees at Hersheypark Arena.

sites had been chosen either. Jean DeAngelis, an occupational health nurse who headed first aid facilities for the Hershey Entertainment and Resorts Company, was having lunch on Friday when she received a call from her employer. State civil defense officials were seeking a safe temporary shelter for evacuees from the region around TMI, and they had chosen the Hersheypark Arena—a 100-foot-high enclosed concrete sports and entertainment venue located in Hershey, about 11 miles from TMI. "I had no idea how many people were involved in the evacuation—they did not give me numbers—but the center was supposed to house all pregnant women,

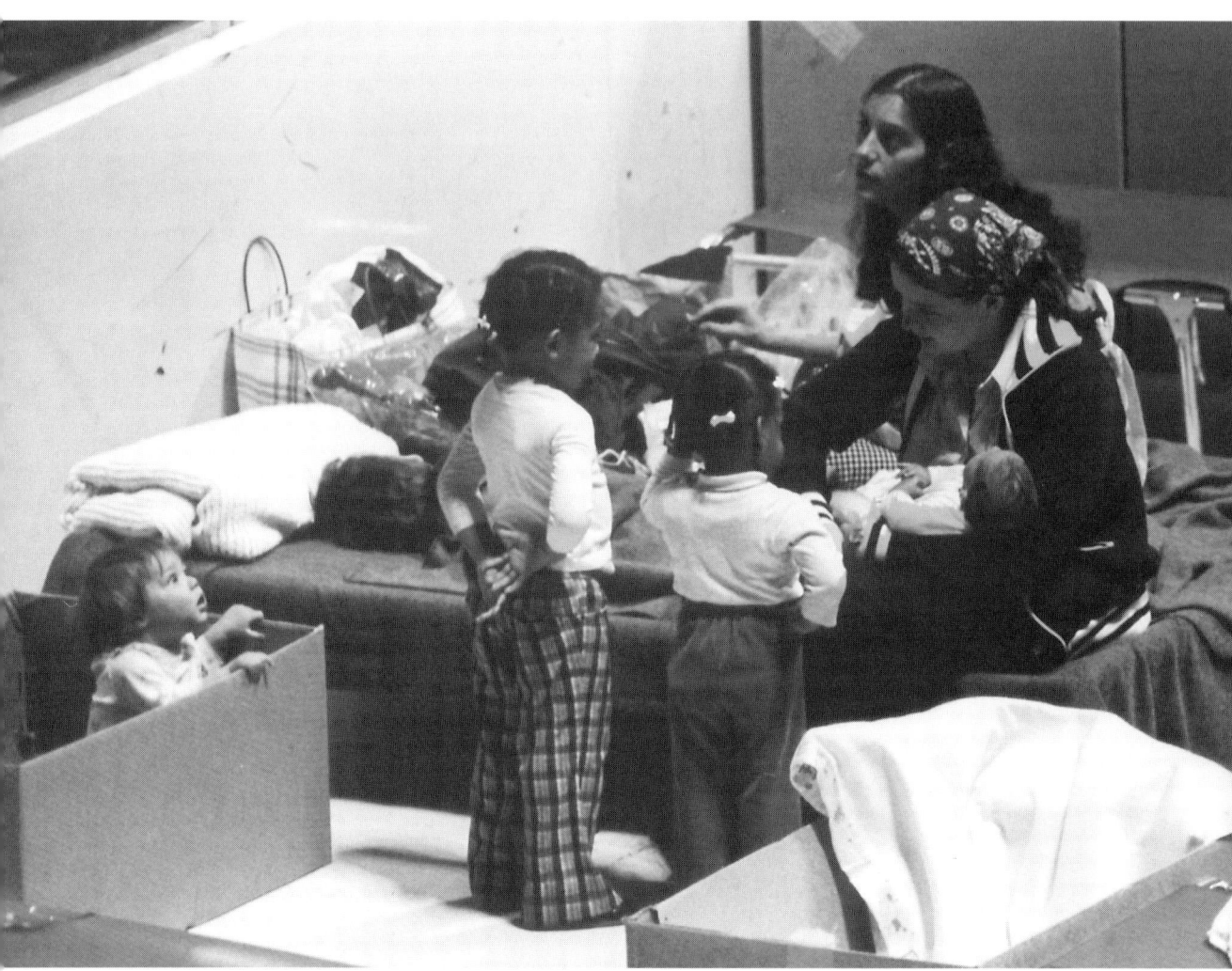

Evacuees gather amid cats and cardboard boxes at the Hersheypark Arena, a concrete structure 11 miles from Three Mile Island.

mothers, and children in the vicinity of Middletown. I knew that would be a lot of people." No one knew how long the evacuation orders would be in effect, so DeAngelis contacted an emergency medical technician (EMT) who had worked for her and asked him to recruit other EMTs. "We needed plenty of people here because we would be on duty 24 hours a day," she remembers. She ordered nine beds moved from the first aid station at nearby Hersheypark for pregnant women who might be about to give birth. (Scores of cots for evacuees would later be delivered by civil defense workers and the Red Cross.) Then she called the Hershey Medical Center to ask doctors and interns to volunteer for shifts at the evacuation site.

Despite the swift planning, none of the medical professionals involved were prepared to handle evacuees who might already be contaminated with radiation. Hersheypark Arena was outfitted with showers and locker rooms for sports events, and DeAngelis believed that at best they might be able to "hose down" victims of radiation contamination. But there was no precedent; a nuclear accident had simply never occurred on this scale before.

Operators inside TMI-2 that Friday morning were unaware of the spreading panic outside the plant until several hours after Jim Floyd ordered the radiation reading above the unit. But as NRC officials on-site analyzed primary coolant samples taken the night before, they discovered another dire situation: the hydrogen bubble that was building up inside the reactor core. Roger Mattson, director of the NRC Division of Systems Safety, believed that the bubble was an immediate threat: it could prevent cooling and eventually lead to a disastrous core meltdown. Already the bubble filled 1,000 cubic feet in the reactor vessel. If the pressure in the system—now holding tenuously—were to drop, the bubble would expand and expose the core once more. Moreover, since only one main coolant pump (of four) was working, there was no backup for the primary cooling system. If that pump failed—and it was being strained almost to the breaking point—Mattson believed that a complete meltdown could occur in less than three hours. He also believed another likelihood. In the extreme heat and highly radioactive atmosphere of the core, the coolant water that had broken down into hydrogen and oxygen might create a highly flammable mixture that could cause an enormous explosion in the reactor vessel or the containment building—a much bigger blast than the one Gary Miller had believed was a valve slamming two days earlier. Mattson wasted no words in his report to NRC chairman Joseph Hendrie: the reactor "was in a condition that no one had anticipated," he said, and added, "I don't know what we are protecting at this point. I think we ought to be moving people."

NRC commissioner Victor Gilinsky was updating President Carter on the situation at TMI, but severe communications problems prevented him from getting "hard numbers" about radiation release rates. Commissioner Hendrie knew that Governor Thornburgh was having the same trouble. Even when the president attempted to call Thornburgh, he could not get through. "We are operating almost totally in the blind, [Thornburgh's] information is ambiguous, mine is nonexistent and . . . it's like a couple of blind men staggering around making decisions," a frustrated Hendrie said.

The president took action. He ordered special phone lines installed so that the White House, the NRC, and the governor's office could communicate freely. Then he asked National Security Advisor Zbigniew Brzezinski to consider having the NRC assume control of the plant, and ordered Harold Denton to fly immediately to Harrisburg to assess the situation. Denton's easygoing and calm demeanor immediately put Thornburgh and Scranton at ease. "[T]he minute he said, 'Hi, I'm Harold Denton,' you know sometimes you have this feeling about people, it just was, this is the right guy," Scranton recalled. Denton set up emergency operations in trailers on the site, and recruited more than 100 specialists from around the country to join him.

In the meantime, however, word of a possible meltdown reached the press. At 4 P.M. on Friday, the newswire service United Press International quoted Bethesda NRC official Dudley Thompson: "We face the ultimate risk of a meltdown, depending on the manner [in which] we cope with the problem." TV stations interrupted regular programming to report the story. White House Press Secretary Jody Powell confirmed the possibility.

Two hours later, CBS *Evening News* anchor Walter Cronkite opened the program with a chilling account:

> Good evening. The world has never known a day quite like today. It faced the considerable uncertainties and dangers of the worst nuclear power plant accident of the atomic age. And the horror tonight is that it could get much worse. It is not an atomic explosion that is feared; the experts say that is impossible. But the specter was raised that perhaps the next most serious kind of nuclear catastrophe, a massive release of radioactivity, [could occur]. The Nuclear Regulatory Commission [stated that] . . . while it is not likely, the potential is there for the ultimate risk of meltdown at the Three Mile Island atomic power plant outside Harrisburg, Pennsylvania.

Denton, however, declared that there was "no imminent danger to the public" from TMI-2. But the conflicting reports coming from Washington, Bethesda, Three Mile Island, and now the national press were hardly reassuring. At 11 P.M. on Friday, Denton called a press conference in an attempt to calm central Pennsylvanians. "We see no possibility of hydrogen explosions in either the containment or the reactor vessel in the near term," he announced. By now, however, even the reporters were near hysteria. "I'm saying to myself, my life, at about 27 years old, is going to be over, because these . . . arrogant utility operators have allowed this thing to run out of control and they're going to kill us," WKBO news director Mike Pintek remembers.

Although the radiation itself was invisible and unknown, the fear of what might be happening was all too palpable to area residents. Many residents noticed the skies that night were filled with an unearthly swirl of oranges, purples, and deep blues. Jean DeAngelis, who by Friday night was receiving the evacuated residents of Middletown at Hersheypark Arena, recalls a similar experience. "I went outside [of the building] for a breath of fresh air, and I don't know whether it had to do with the radiation, but there was a very eerie light in the sky," she remembers.

By Saturday morning, March 31, Governor Thornburgh was once more faced with deciding whether to declare a general evacuation of the area—an order that would involve moving 400,000 people, including invalids and hospital patients. While he hesitated to do so without accumulating all the facts, he also realized that a full evacuation of even five miles' radius from the power plant was an enormous undertaking. "We were making plans for the evacuation not only of people, but of government, of how we were going to govern in the case of the massive meltdown and escape of radioactivity," Lieutenant Governor Bill Scranton explained in 1999. But Thornburgh had received some reassuring news: in an effort to lend steadiness to the conflicting information about the safety of TMI, President Jimmy Carter announced that he would be paying a visit to the crippled plant the following day.

As soon as Carter arrived in Harrisburg with his wife, Rosalynn, and 16 White House correspondents, Denton briefed the president on the status of TMI-2, and then the two men and the First Lady toured the unit. Carter had served under Admiral Hyman Rickover as a naval officer, and had personal experience with nuclear power plants. Nearly 30 years before, he was one of the volunteer workers who dismantled a damaged reactor at the Chalk River

"THE WORLD HAS NEVER KNOWN A DAY QUITE LIKE TODAY" 87

President Carter (center right), Governor Richard Thornburgh (wearing glasses behind Carter), and Dr. Harold Denton (left of Thornburgh) tour the control room of TMI-2.

nuclear plant in Ontario, Canada. Still, one of the greatest difficulties Denton faced was sorting out the confusion over the state of the hydrogen bubble in the reactor core. Two highly respected nuclear experts—Roger Mattson and Victor Stello, director of the NRC Office of Inspection and Enforcement—were at odds over the level of imminent danger from the bubble. Stello was certain that Mattson's calculations predicting an imminent explosion contained some kind of flaw, but he could not determine what it was. In any event, he believed the situation was far less perilous than Mattson was declaring—and he was angered that Mattson was contributing to the panic over the accident. The two exchanged heated words just minutes before Carter's arrival. Whatever the truth, Denton believed that the president needed to hear both scenarios.

President Carter urged Denton and other NRC officials to be conservative in their statements to the public to avoid further panic—and he effectively muzzled Met Ed representatives, who had consistently presented conflicting information since the day of the accident. That afternoon, Carter called a joint press conference with Governor Thornburgh to address local residents. "[I]f it does become necessary, your governor . . . will ask you and others in this area to take appropriate actions to ensure your safety. . . . This will not indicate that the danger is high," Carter emphasized. "It will indicate that a change is being made in the operation of the cooling water system to permanently correct the present state of the reactor, and it is strictly a precautionary measure."

Middletown mayor Robert Reid expressed the vast relief that he and other central Pennsylvanians felt upon hearing Carter's reassuring words. "It was really a shot in the arm," he explains. "Did you ever see people like they're ready to laugh but ready to cry at the same time?"

By 7:00 P.M. on Sunday, April 1, NRC officials learned that there was no danger of explosion in TMI-2. Mattson had based his figures on hydrogen's behavior in an unpressurized containment vessel, but the pressure in Unit 2's core was holding at 1,000 pounds per square inch. Victor Stello had been correct. Under such conditions, there was no chance that oxygen could spark a deadly explosion of the hydrogen bubble.

Two hours after Carter and Thornburgh's press conference, the bubble had shrunk by almost two-thirds, to just 350 cubic feet. By Monday morning, April 2, the bubble was only half that size. There would be no general evacuation. As a precaution, however, Governor Thornburgh kept the evacuation recommendation in force until NRC officials determined when a "cold shutdown" of Unit 2 (in which the core is cooled by the natural movement of water rather than by mechanical pumping) could be achieved.

By Friday, April 6, PEMA estimated that 90 percent of Pennsylvanians who had fled the vicinity of Three Mile Island had returned home. On April 9, Governor Thornburgh officially lifted his March 30 advisory. The long nightmare, it appeared, was finally over.

These boxes contain contaminated tools used in the cleanup of TMI-2. They will remain radioactive for thousands of years.

A Legacy of Fear

After the accident at TMI, the federal government required local meetings in which citizens living near nuclear power plants were provided the opportunity to speak with NRC officials, plant representatives, and their own elected officials. Kari Light, a Ph.D. and resident of Middletown, was one of the enraged locals who attended a Middletown, Pennsylvania, council meeting on June 20, 1979, less than four months after the accident:

> I have lived here literally since before I was born. My mother was pregnant here. And this has always been a safe, secure place for me. Like a lot of other people, when I was young and silly, I left town and I was away for a while; but I came back because this is where I felt I

belonged, where I felt safe.... That is gone....

I work with children. Part of what I do is play therapy with children. And I love them.... That also is gone. I can't look at children the way I could two or three months ago. I look at them and wonder what's going to happen to them. I wonder which ones of them are going to be able to produce children and which ones are not. I wonder which ones of them are going to have leukemia when they are older; I look at them and I grieve for them.... I'm grieving for your children, and you should be doing something about it.

For most residents of the counties surrounding Three Mile Island, the accident at TMI could not have been more terrifying. But the ordeal did not end with Unit 2's shutdown. Instead, it left lasting psychological, emotional—and some say even physical—effects. "There had never been anything like this," Bill Scranton explained 20 years later. "[I]t wasn't something you could see or feel or taste or touch. We were talking about radiation, which generated an enormous amount of fear."

By the time TMI-2 began producing power in 1978, most residents were accustomed to the huge plant and its looming cooling towers. Although several antinuclear citizens' groups had mobilized in Pennsylvania against the construction of the new plant, most locals had initially believed it was perfectly safe. Met Ed's Blain Fabian issued weekly press releases on the plant, but the information was so technical that most reporters could not understand it. "What had been an attempt to produce information in the public interest served instead to desensitize the local press to problems at Three Mile Island," observed Mark

Stephens, author of *Three Mile Island*. In fact, TMI-2 had been plagued with problems ever since it went critical (began a nuclear reaction) exactly a year before the accident, on March 28, 1978.

Both TMI reactors were designed and built by Babcock & Wilcox, but the plumbing, cooling, safety, and control systems were built by two different companies. GPU chose engineering firm Burns & Roe to design the systems for TMI-2, in part for economic reasons: the cost of the TMI-2 project had quadrupled to almost $800 million since its 1972 groundbreaking. Met Ed engineers had serious concerns about GPU's decision, however. The model for Unit 2 was an adaptation of the salt-water–cooled Oyster Creek plant on the New Jersey coast, but TMI's plant relied on the freshwater Susquehanna River for its cooling system. The PWR in Unit 2 was a streamlined version used at several other U.S. nuclear power facilities, and included a so-called once-through steam generator, which was smaller, more efficient, and cheaper to build than most others. However, because this model kept the steam at a higher temperature, it was also more likely to boil dry.

Additionally, turbine and reactor safety systems on this model were not interconnected. This made a reactor scram less likely in the event of a "transient" (abnormal condition or event) in the system, saving the unit expensive downtime. But it also required that reactor pressure be more carefully monitored—and relied heavily on the reliability of the ERV. Before Unit 2 went on-line (began providing commercial power) on December 30, 1978, it had been down for repairs and maintenance 195 out of 274 days—a rate of 71 percent—and the reactor had scrammed 10 times.

Local residents knew little about these problems, but they did know that the final cost of the plant far exceeded the original estimate. They could see the results of Met Ed's budget overrun in their monthly electric bills. They also learned through local newspapers that Met Ed may have rushed to get TMI-2 on-line before the end of 1978 to qualify for roughly $40 million in tax credits. In August 1978, an independent tabloid called *Harrisburg* had published a shocking fictitious scenario of a major LOCA at Three Mile Island that sent deadly radioactive plumes shooting into the sky above the area, killing everything within miles. When central Pennsylvanians first heard about the accident on March 28, 1979, that hypothetical situation suddenly seemed a very real possibility.

After the accident, Met Ed president Walter Creitz admitted that the company gained tax advantages by getting TMI-2 into commercial operation before 1979. But he consistently denied that they had cut corners where safety was concerned. Still, the down rate (time off-line) for the unit was 30 points higher than the industry average for new plant operations, and many of the problems that occurred before March 28 were similar to those that caused the accident itself. For example, the ERV on the pressurizer vessel had failed on October 13, 1978, causing a reactor scram; six more scrams occurred before the end of that year. The valve failure had occurred at other nuclear power plants as well: in March 1977, an ERV at the Davis-Besse plant near Toledo, Ohio, stuck open during a scram. Fortunately, operators noticed the malfunction before the reactor (also a Babcock & Wilcox design) suffered major damage.

In the aftermath of the Three Mile Island accident,

Met Ed faced a cleanup project of mammoth proportions. The first step was to bleed off the hydrogen bubble that had caused so much alarm. By manipulating pressure levels in the reactor, operators broke up the hydrogen so that the coolant carried it in small bubbles to the pressurizer vessel. The hydrogen was released when the coolant was sprayed into the vessel, and then escaped into the containment building and was recombined with oxygen and turned into water. For this last step, Met Ed operators needed access to the auxiliary building, where highly radioactive coolant overflow had been stored. The company ordered tons of lead bricks, which were flown in on C-131 cargo planes; workers fixed the lead in place over the recombiner control panels to shield operators from radiation contamination.

The cleanup of the damaged reactor at TMI-2 was one of the most technically challenging efforts in U.S. engineering history. Every surface had to be decontaminated, and all water used for the process had to be carefully handled. Crews processed and stored more than 2.8 million gallons of radioactive coolant from the accident itself (it was later evaporated under special procedures). Most important, 100 metric tons of uranium had to be removed from the site entirely without causing additional hazards to the public or to the more than 1,000 workers involved in the cleanup. This procedure, called defueling, required that the damaged uranium remain underwater at all times.

Not until July 1982 were radiation levels in the reactor core safe enough for people to enter the containment building. Workers clad in bright yellow antiradiation suits and armed with dosimeters lowered a remote-control camera into the reactor core.

The cleanup of TMI-2 was one of the most challenging engineering efforts in U.S. history. Every surface needed to be decontaminated. This worker suits up in protective gear for the cleanup effort.

The images displayed on television were stunning. For the first time, the world got a glimpse of how close TMI-2 had come to a complete meltdown. Where the tops of the 12-foot-high fuel rods once stood in a tight bundle, there was nothing. "As the camera was lowered down into the reactor vessel, it went deeper and deeper . . . and where's the core?

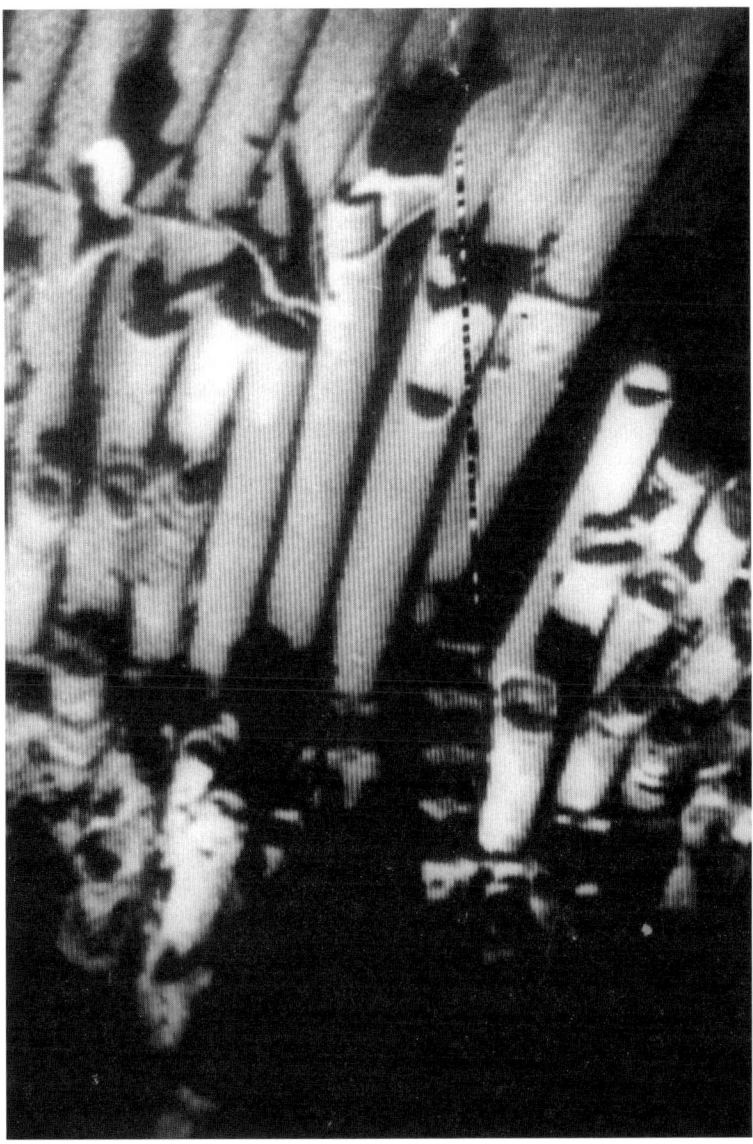

Radiation levels kept workers out of the containment building until July 1982. Only then could workers get a glimpse of the inside of the reactor. This view from a remote-control camera shows the damaged fuel assemblies in TMI-2's damaged core.

There is no core," Harold Denton remembers thinking. "We've gone down four, five, six feet." Nearly 50 percent of the fuel rods had melted or crumbled. "I just didn't realize at the time how severely the core had been damaged," said Denton in 2001. "I took away the feeling that we had been complacent. . . . And it was a wakeup call for the nuclear industry."

In October 1985, workers stood on a platform above the perimeter of TMI-2's reactor vessel and used long-handled tools to lift the damaged fuel into canisters hanging below the platform. The fuel filled 342 canisters, which were shipped to the federal government's Idaho National Laboratory for storage. In 1990, the fuel transfer was complete; the following year, the remaining coolant was pumped out of TMI-2's system, and in December 1993—14 years after the accident—the NRC granted GPU a license to place Unit 2 in Post-Defueling Monitored Storage. The reactor will never operate again.

GPU, the parent company of Met Ed (now defunct), still owns TMI-2. Unit 1 was purchased in December 1999 by AmerGen, a joint venture of the Philadelphia-based PECO Energy Company and the British Energy Company of Edinburgh, Scotland. The deal was the first outright sale of a commercial nuclear reactor in the United States. TMI-1, which was shut down for refueling at the time of the accident, remained out of commission in the wake of the crisis and was not restarted until 1985. It received poor safety ratings by the NRC in 1998, but AmerGen earned high marks for improving the ratings in 2000. The NRC operating license for the TMI-1 plant expires in 2014; at that time, both units will be decommissioned (removed from service).

In April 1979, President Carter appointed a 12-member commission to investigate the cause of the accident at Three Mile Island and determine its effects on the health and safety of residents and plant workers. The commission, headed by Dartmouth College president John Kemeny, submitted its findings in October 1979. Among its primary recommendations were (1) that the nuclear power industry

John Kemeny tours the control room of TMI-2. Kemeny was appointed by President Carter to head a 12-member commission that investigated the causes of the accident.

establish and enforce standards of safety and operation; (2) that each utility company establish a department solely for nuclear operations; (3) that each nuclear power plant regularly gather, review, and analyze data on operator experience and assess risks of specific types of incidents, such as loss-of-coolant accidents, multiple errors, or human failure; (4) that utilities establish NRC-accredited training institutions for nuclear plant operators and supervisors; (5) that utilities maintain research on the effects of low-level radiation and establish emergency radiation programs; (6) that utilities "detail

(continued on page 102)

CHERNOBYL: AN ONGOING DISASTER

On April 28, 1986, an alarm sounded at Forsmark nuclear power plant near Stockholm, Sweden. Workers evacuated the plant while technicians searched for the leak, but they found none. That day, Finland, Norway, and Denmark announced strangely high radiation levels that tests revealed were consistent with a nuclear reactor fire. By afternoon, scientists examining weather patterns over Europe pinpointed the probable source: Chernobyl, a nuclear power plant in the Ukraine, then part of the Soviet Union. At 9:00 P.M., a Soviet news source announced "an accident" at Chernobyl, but maintained that "measures [were] being taken to eliminate the consequences."

What the news report called an accident was actually the worst nuclear disaster in history, more devastating by far than the 1979 crisis at Three Mile Island. Worse yet, the announcement came nearly three days after the accident actually occurred at Chernobyl-4's 1,000-MW reactor. On April 26, workers conducted an unauthorized low-level operations test, an extremely dangerous procedure for a graphite-moderated RBMK reactor (a type of boiling-water reactor). Chernobyl's units were designed not only to produce electricity but also to manufacture military-grade plutonium; its multiple functions did not allow for a containment building. In all other countries that use nuclear power, the required containment shell is an important protection against radiation releases.

Compounding the problem, during the low-level test the technicians disabled safety features that would have shut down the reactor before it reached dangerous levels. The power level in the reactor surged to 100 times normal, and at 1:23 A.M. it exploded twice, blowing off the roof of the structure. The graphite inside the core ignited, and the plume of intense radioactivity that shot into the atmosphere was so huge that it blew across the Ukraine into northern and eastern Europe. This was the fallout that Swedish technicians discovered two days later, 1,000 miles northwest of Chernobyl.

Thirty-one people died immediately in the blast, and the graphite burned for nine days. Radiation levels were so high that pilots sent up to douse the fire with barium received lethal doses. Many of the soldiers brought in to fight the fire on the ground became seriously ill or died soon afterward. Yet astonishingly, Soviet authorities issued no immediate evacuation orders. In Kiev, about 65 miles south of Chernobyl, May Day parades took place as scheduled. In Chernobyl and the nearby town of Pripyat,

A LEGACY OF FEAR 101

This is an aerial view of Chernobyl taken a few days after the massive explosion and fire. The hole in the structure is where the reactor exploded. This was the world's worst nuclear accident.

people played soccer outdoors. Not until a week after the accident was a roughly 20-mile area around the plant cleared out; the evacuation of 135,000 people within that region took two months to complete. The heavily contaminated area measured almost 11,000 square miles, nearly two-thirds of which is in neighboring Belarus.

Incredibly, the Chernobyl plant resumed partial operation in October 1986—a calculated attempt by the Soviet government to prove that the accident was not as severe as believed. Estimates of health problems caused by the accident vary widely. Soviet authorities kept the official death toll at 31, despite the fact that 5,000 to 7,000 cleanup workers died of radiation poisoning by 1990. Predictions about rising cancer rates also vary; the Ukrainian Ministry of Health claims that 125,000 of its citizens have died directly or indirectly from the accident; others argue that that number is inflated to encourage financial aid to the Ukraine and that the actual number is closer to 14.

The Chernobyl plant continued operating until December 2000. A huge concrete "sarcophagus" was built over Chernobyl-4 in 1986. Authorities claimed it would last indefinitely. Within five years, the structure developed cracks. If it is not rebuilt it may collapse, spewing radioactive dust into the atmosphere once more.

(continued from page 99)

clearly and consistently the actions public officials and utilities should take in the event of off-site radiation doses resulting from release of radioactivity."

Perhaps most important, the commission emphasized that a "change in attitude" toward safety and regulation issues was in order within the nuclear power industry. Company officials had an obligation to educate the public about plant operations and about the possibility of radiation exposure, the report said. It also declared what it called the "public right to information": the right of residents in each plant's vicinity to receive clear, timely, and accurate information from plant officials, especially during emergencies.

The NRC also commissioned an investigation into the TMI-2 accident, headed by an attorney named Mitchell Rogovin. The Rogovin Report, published in 1980, agreed with the findings of the Kemeny Commission and suspended the issuance of nuclear plant construction permits and operating licenses. In September 1980, the NRC lifted its temporary suspension and issued the first full-power operating license since the TMI accident. In the decade afterward, it granted operating licenses to more than 40 other reactors, but since the disaster at Three Mile Island, no construction permits for nuclear reactors have been issued.

The nuclear power industry itself, under intense public and government scrutiny after the crisis, launched its own efforts at reform. Around the time that President Carter appointed the Kemeny Commission, utility executives recruited the nonprofit Electric Power Research Institute (EPRI) to launch a study of the events at TMI. The EPRI's formation of the Nuclear Safety Analysis Center was a source of technical and safety information for both the Kemeny and the Rogovin Commissions. In December 1979, nuclear industry executives established the self-policing Institute of Nuclear Power Operations (INPO), aimed at promoting "the highest levels of safety and reliability in the operation of nuclear power plants." In 1985, following the recommendations of the federal reports, the INPO established the National Academy for Nuclear Training for accreditation of key nuclear plant employees.

In all, the cleanup of the crippled TMI-2 reactor lasted 12 years and cost more than $1 billion. Like the unseen radiation itself, however, another kind of toll was exacted: area residents were left with potent feelings of anxiety, distrust, and seething anger, not only from the accident itself but from the bewildering and contradictory information that corporate, state, and federal officials issued during the crisis. Perhaps the most infuriating irony was the fact that Met Ed customers would be forced to help shoulder the financial burden of the accident that caused them so much anguish. Met Ed relied on Three Mile Island to provide 40 percent of its power; with Unit 2 out of commission it was forced to purchase higher-priced power elsewhere—and it passed on the expense to its customers, some of whom lived in New Jersey, far from the plant itself. Worse yet, a portion of the cleanup cost itself was added to customer bills. In a 1979 multipart series on the events at Three Mile Island, the *Washington Post* interviewed central Pennsylvanians about their feelings toward the nuclear industry. "The people around Three Mile Island had generally been boosters of nuclear power, but the accident in their back yards brought a change in attitude," it said. "If our faith in Met Ed is shaken," wrote the *Middletown Press and Journal* in a front-page editorial, "our belief in the entire nuclear power industry also rides on thin ice."

Mistrust of the industry and anger over the widespread misinformation during the TMI crisis were not the only concerns in the aftermath of the accident. Even today, many residents have a lingering fear that they may have been exposed to radiation levels high enough to cause permanent health problems, affect plant and animal life, and contribute to higher rates of birth defects. State, federal, and industry authorities disagreed not only about the actual amounts of radiation released during the accident but also on what level might cause health problems. The NRC points out that studies conducted by the commission itself; the Environmental Protection Agency; the Department of Health, Education, and Welfare (now Health and Human Services); the Department of Energy; the Commonwealth of Pennsylvania; and a number of independent organizations have shown that "the average dose [of radiation] to about two million people in the area was only about one millirem. . . . Compared to the natural radioactive background dose of about 100–125 millirem[s] per year for the area," the NRC concludes, "the maximum dose to a person at the site boundary would have been less than 100 millirem[s]."

In the years after the accident, scientists collected thousands of air, water, milk, plant, soil, and food samples from the area. Between 1981 and 1991, the Pennsylvania Department of Health conducted at least seven major studies. They included reports on infant death rates, the incidence of hypothyroidism (an autoimmune disease that is sometimes linked to radiation exposure), the incidence and mortality

These Environmental Protection Agency workers are examining locations of water samples that measure radioactivity from the area around the TMI accident.

rates of various cancers, and the possible link between radiation or psychological stress and adverse pregnancy outcomes (like fetal abnormalities or deaths). The most recent studies, conducted in 1991, examined the incidence of cancer among people who lived within five miles of the plant and among women of childbearing age who lived within 10 miles of the plant in 1979. None of these studies detected increases in disease or death rates. Based on these reports, the NRC concludes that the accident caused "negligible effects on the physical health of individuals or the environment."

Other studies, however, have produced different results. A 1991 joint report by Columbia University researchers and the National Audubon Society suggested that increased stress, not radioactivity, may have caused higher incidences of cancer among residents closest to the plant. A controversial 1997 report by researchers at the University of North Carolina at Chapel Hill concluded that increased rates of lung cancer and leukemia near the TMI plant suggest that radiation releases during the accident were much higher than believed.

In June 1996, Harrisburg U.S. District Court Judge Sylvia Rambo dismissed a class action lawsuit by area residents against Met Ed and GPU alleging that the accident at TMI caused adverse health effects. Judge Rambo claimed that the plaintiffs failed to show evidence that the dosimeters used to monitor radiation levels were inadequate. She also declared that the maximum off-site exposure was about 100 millirems, and that the plaintiffs could not prove that there were unreported hydrogen explosions that caused concentrated releases of radioactivity during the crisis. (As of 2001, the plaintiffs in the lawsuit were appealing the ruling.)

Whether central Pennsylvanians agree with the health findings, no one disputes the immense psychological and emotional impact of the TMI accident. Dr. Jane Bratz, chief of the Pennsylvania Department of Health's Three Mile Island Health Research Program, says that the mental ordeal of surviving the crisis may have caused people to perceive their own physical health as worsened, even where medical records showed otherwise. Many local residents who

A LEGACY OF FEAR

This Environmental Protection Agency device measures radioactivity in the area of TMI-2. Many studies have been conducted on water, soil, livestock, and food products from the area. None of them have shown any danger from radiation.

lived near TMI in 1979 also feared contamination of plants and animals. "I try not to buy anything [produced in] Pennsylvania anymore," said Nancy Prelesnik, who in 1980 lived in Hershey. "I always question things at the grocery stores, and they think you're crazy to want to know where you're getting your produce." Jane Lee, a dairy farmer four miles from Three Mile Island, noticed that in the summer of 1979 the normally plentiful species of birds in her area seemed to disappear. She also noted that the trees on her land were almost completely defoliated by the end of the summer, and that by fall some were showing "several growing seasons at once." Botanists told her the problem was not disease or infestation, but they could not say for sure what caused it. On another dairy farm 5.5 miles from TMI, Clair Hoover claimed that he lost seven cows and 13 calves when his cattle began aborting and dying in the week after the accident. Despite laboratory findings to the contrary, Hoover believes that high radiation releases caused the losses.

Even some who visited the area during the TMI crisis were anxious about being in proximity to a nuclear power plant that seemed out of control. John Baer, who worked for the Hershey public television station WITF-TV, remembers the trepidation outsiders felt when arriving there. "We interviewed Nina Tottenberg of National Public Radio on one of our shows," Baer said the year after the accident. "She said that she knew reporters who had spent a year in Saigon [during the Vietnam War] and had turned down this assignment." Mike Gray, author of *The China Syndrome* screenplay and an observer of the unfolding events of March and April, 1979, describes the horror he felt at the thought of a full-blown meltdown: " [W]e would now no longer be able to drive through the city of Harrisburg," he said in 1999. "The Pennsylvania Turnpike would have to go north through Scranton. And . . . within a hundred-mile radius of this plant you have Philadelphia, Baltimore, Washington, D.C. . . . [We] were that close to a disaster of almost unimaginable proportions."

"I never thought I would feel like a refugee in my own country in peace time," Nancy Prelesnik said in 1980. Still, like many other residents of south-central Pennsylvania, she has noticed a positive consequence of the accident. "[It] has done a strange thing to our community," she said. "You see how much one person can count. . . . The [good] qualities start coming out in people, people that have gone through this Godawful, horrible crap, this nightmare. . . . These people know it."

What the Future Holds

In an effort to prevent accidents like the one at TMI, the NRC has instituted the use of reactor simulators. Here, a reactor operator trains at a simulator.

In September 1999, a uranium processing plant in Tokaimura, Japan, 80 miles northeast of Tokyo, experienced an uncontrolled nuclear reaction when workers handling uranium-235 were jolted by a bright blue flash of light. The three workers handling the uranium sustained serious injuries; 34 others were heavily contaminated. Although the reaction was brought under control within 20 hours, it placed 300,000 people in the vicinity around Tokaimura at risk. An investigation revealed that it was the result of safety violations by workers who were mixing uranium with nitric acid to produce fuel.

Although the incident was far different in scope and cause from the accident at Three Mile Island, it highlighted the continuing safety concerns of a country that increasingly relies upon nuclear energy for power supplies. "This is an accident that's so basic it should never have happened," Japanese antinuclear activist Chihiro Kamisawa said at the time. "So much has been made of Japan's sophisticated technology that supposedly makes nuclear energy safe. The accident proves that's absolutely not true."

Japan is not alone in its quest for new power sources. The International Energy Agency predicts that the world's energy demand will increase 65 percent by 2020. It estimates that at present, more than 400 operating nuclear reactors worldwide serve more than one billion people, mostly in Europe and the United Kingdom. In the United States—even though no new plants have been commissioned since the TMI accident—nuclear energy accounts for about 20 percent of power production.

In the days after the Japanese accident, U.S. and British officials in particular took pains to dismiss the possibility of a similar accident occurring in their countries. Both nations pointed out that procedures have been put in place to minimize one of the most unpredictable and common causes of nuclear accidents: human error and mismanagement. This is especially true in the United States, where in the wake of Three Mile Island one of the main goals for improving the safety and efficiency of nuclear power plants has been to better train operators for unexpected emergencies.

Since 1979, the NRC has expanded its review program to ensure that at least two nuclear power inspectors live near and work in each plant in the country. It has also retooled its operator training and staffing requirements and established fitness-for-duty programs to guard against alcohol and other drug abuse by workers. The NRC has required plant engineers to improve instrumentation so that operators can more easily detect problems and take proper measures to prevent accidents. Together with industry groups, it promoted the increased use of reactor simulators and a more careful assessment of control rooms and instrumentation.

New reactor designs that incorporate advanced computer systems and better-controlled fission processes have also increased the safety and efficiency of nuclear power since the accident at TMI. Of the next-generation reactor designs submitted to the NRC, three have been approved for possible licensing in the United States: the Advanced Boiling-Water reactor (ABWR), designed by GE and approved in August 1997; the System 80+ reactor, designed by Westinghouse and approved in June 1998; and the AP600 reactor, also by Westinghouse and approved in March 2000.

As the name suggests, the ABWR is an improved version of the BWRs used in Europe, Japan, and the United States today. The System 80+ and the AP600 reactors are modified versions of first-generation PWRs. They include improvements to the ECCS, feedwater pumps, and decay heat removal systems—three components of TMI's Unit 2 that contributed to the 1979 accident.

Nine other reactor designs have been submitted to the NRC, but only two are being considered: the AP1000, a larger version of the AP600; and Exelon's Pebble Bed Module Reactor (PBMR), a gas-cooled reactor that cannot physically meltdown and so does not require an ECCS. Even opponents of nuclear power concede that the design offers far greater safety than that of first-generation plants because it does not require an active reactor; that is, one in which the continuous fission process requires a complicated and possibly dangerous procedure to reach shutdown. PBMRs will only begin the fission process when heated helium is added to the reactor core. When the flow of helium stops, so does the reaction—and the core cools itself naturally. Exelon says that other advantages to the PBMR include its scaled-down size and the fact that it produces only about one-tenth the power of most current plants. This modular design will enable technicians to run 10 PBMRs from one control room.

Next-generation nuclear reactor designs come at a time when energy concerns dominate political and environmental discussions in the United States. Two bills introduced to Congress in 2001—the National Energy Security Act and the Nuclear Energy Electricity Assurance Act—offer incentives for more-efficient nuclear power production and encourage research and development of the technology, so that America can avoid inadequate power supplies in the wake of power deregulation problems. Still, the Kyoto Protocol—a 1997 international treaty that calls for the reduction of emissions to seven percent below 1990 levels by 2008—has rejected nuclear power industry officials' claims that nuclear energy can help reduce global warming.

Whatever the future of nuclear energy may be, the horror of what might have happened during the accident at Three Mile Island on March 28, 1979 will not soon be forgotten. The crisis that emerged that week on a small Susquehanna River island transformed the nuclear power industry not only in the United States, but also around the globe. For the first time since the technology was developed in the late 1940s and early 1950s, the world realized that it was not the foolproof energy solution proponents had dreamed it might be.

Mike Gray, a trained engineer, author of *The China Syndrome* and coauthor of *The Warning,* a book about the TMI accident, recalls questioning NRC inspector Bob Pollard about the events that led to the partial meltdown. "Pollard said, 'The serious accidents never occur out of the blue. There's always some kind of a warning. This was a warning.' . . . The lesson that we must learn from

WHAT THE FUTURE HOLDS

Three Mile Island is that . . . we have created a technology here which is very unforgiving," Gray said in 1999. "We were fortunate."

NBC News correspondent Robert Hager was sent to Three Mile Island on Friday, March 30, the day Governor Thornburgh recommended a limited evacuation of pregnant women and children. As he stepped off the plane at the Harrisburg International Airport, he heard the wail of the sirens that someone had set off in Harrisburg. "It may have been a sort of false alarm at the time," Hager remembered 20 years later, "but long-term, it sounded an end to an era when we believed that nuclear power would be the answer to the world's energy problems."

The accident at Three Mile Island on March 28, 1979, transformed the nuclear power industry around the globe. For the first time, the world realized that it was not the foolproof energy solution proponents had dreamed it might be.

Chronology

Monday, March 26, 1979

A plant worker at Three Mile Island closes both of Unit 2's twelve valves during a routine maintenance check

Wednesday, March 28, 1979

4:00 A.M.: Residents near the Three Mile Island nuclear power plant are awakened by the roar of a jet of steam shooting from Unit 2; inside the plant, a small amount of water in the instrument air system had caused a reactor scram and turbine trip. The Electromatic relief valve (ERV) on the pressurizer vessel becomes stuck open; coolant begins draining from the reactor core

4:02 A.M.: The steam generators begin to boil dry; the feedwater circuit can no longer remove heat from the reactor

4:03 A.M.: Two high-pressure injection pumps, part of the emergency core cooling system (ECCS), automatically begin pumping water into the primary cooling system

4:05 A.M.: Control room operators notice that the reactor's temperature is level; operators shut down one of the high-pressure pumps and reduce the flow in the other

4:07 A.M.: Fearful that the reactor is going solid, operators shut down the second high-pressure pump

4:08 A.M.: Operators realize that no water is reaching the steam generators from the feedwater circuit; they discover the twelves are closed and immediately open them

4:11 A.M.: An alarm indicates that the quench tank has overflowed and the containment building is filling with water; the sump water is automatically pumped into the auxiliary building

4:40 A.M.: Workers realize the water draining into the auxiliary building is radioactive and they stop the transfer and shut down the sump pump; by this time, steam from the water in the building has already vented into the atmosphere

Chronology

5:00 A.M.: Pipes in the primary cooling circuit begin to cavitate from the steam pockets building in them; the reactor begins to boil dry

5:20–5:40 A.M.: Operators shut down one set of primary cooling pumps; 20 minutes later, the other set of pumps shut down automatically. The cooling system is at a near standstill

6:00 A.M.: Detectors in the containment building measure increased levels of radiation

6:15 A.M.: The water level in the reactor vessel drops below the top of the core; the core has begun to melt

6:22 A.M.: The ERV is closed after 2 hours and 22 minutes

6:56–7:00 A.M.: Unknown to operators, the reactor core is two-thirds exposed; Bill Zewe declares a site emergency; local authorities and plant owner Met Ed are notified

7:24 A.M.: A monitor in the containment building shows radiation shining through the reactor vessel; Gary Miller declares a general emergency

8:25 A.M.: Local radio station WKBO reports a general emergency at TMI

8:45 A.M.: NRC inspectors head to TMI from King of Prussia, PA; federal and local agencies are notified of the situation at TMI

9:00–10:00 A.M.: National Security Council office is informed of the situation; President Carter is briefed

10:30 A.M.: Radiation in the containment dome soars to 40,000 to 50,000 rems per hour; Miller opens the motorized blocking valve on the pressurizer, causing more coolant to leave the reactor. A hydrogen bubble forms at the top of the reactor; some escapes into the containment building

11:00 A.M.: Lieutenant Governor Bill Scranton holds a press conference declaring "no danger to public health and safety" from the TMI incident

Chronology

2:00 P.M.: The hydrogen bubble ignites; operators hear what sounds like a valve slamming and see a sudden pressure spike in the reactor

4:30 P.M.: Scranton calls a second press conference announcing a "release of radioactivity into the environment"

Thursday, March 29, 1979

11:00 A.M.: Congressman John Wydler and Lieutenant Governor Bill Scranton tour Unit 2's auxiliary building; Met Ed holds a contentious press conference and denies any danger to the public

4:00 P.M.: Governor Dick Thornburgh calls a press conference and assures the public that "there is no cause for alarm"

Friday, March 30, 1979

7:35–8:15 A.M.: TMI-2 shift supervisor Jim Floyd vents radioactive gas into the air above the plant and notifies PEMA; level is measured at 1,200 millirems. Based on incomplete information, the NRC notifies Governor Thornburgh and the White House of a potential uncontrolled release of radiation

10:00 A.M.: The governor urges everyone within 10 miles of Three Mile Island to stay indoors until further notice

11:15 A.M.: Air-raid sirens are set off in Harrisburg

11:30 A.M.: Met Ed vice president Jack Herbein insists that conditions at TMI are "stable"

12:30 P.M.: Thornburgh advises pregnant women and preschool children within a five-mile radius of TMI to evacuate. The order sets off a panic and 140,000 people leave the area over the next few days

4:00 P.M.: The national press receives word of a "possible meltdown" at TMI

11:00 P.M.: Harold Denton, sent to Harrisburg by President Carter, assures the public that the 1,000-cubic-foot hydrogen bubble in the reactor is not in danger of igniting

Chronology

Saturday, March 31, 1979

    Governor Thornburgh considers issuing a full evacuation order for the area around TMI; the hydrogen bubble is still inside the Unit 2 reactor vessel

Sunday, April 1, 1979

    President Jimmy Carter and his wife, Rosalynn, arrive in Harrisburg and tour the TMI-2 plant; the president holds a joint press conference with Governor Thornburgh to calm public fears about radiation dangers

    7:00 P.M.: NRC officials learn there is no danger of explosion from the hydrogen bubble, which has shrunk to 350 cubic feet

Monday, April 2, 1979

    The hydrogen bubble continues to shrink to 175 cubic feet; Thornburgh determines no evacuation orders are necessary but leaves the evacuation advisory in effect

Friday, April 6, 1979

    PEMA estimates that 90 percent of Pennsylvanians who fled the vicinity of Three Mile Island have returned home

Monday, April 9, 1979

    Governor Thornburgh officially lifts the March 30 evacuation advisory

Further Reading

Books and Periodicals

Del Tredici, Robert. *The People of Three Mile Island.* San Francisco: Sierra Club Books, 1980.

Lampton, Christopher. *Nuclear Accident.* Brookfield, Conn.: Millbrook Press, 1992.

Larimer, Tim. "The Japan Syndrome." *TIME,* October 11, 1999.

Stephens, Mark. *Three Mile Island.* New York: Random House, 1980.

Websites

CNN.com
  "Three Mile Island: 20 Years Later"
  images.cnn.com/US/9903/28/3mile.anniversary/

Federal Emergency Management Agency (FEMA) for Kids
  www.fema.gov/kids/

Marshall Brain's How Stuff Works
  "How Nuclear Power Works"
  www.howstuffworks.com/nuclear-power.htm

  "How Nuclear Radiation Works"
  www.howstuffworks.com/nuclear.htm

MSNBC.com
  "Environment: Three Mile Island: 20 Years Later"
  www.msnbc.com/news/253397.asp

National Academy of Engineering
  "Greatest Engineering Achievements of the 20th Century"
  www.greatachievements.org/greatachievements/index.html

PBS: The American Experience—Meltdown at Three Mile Island
  www.pbs.org/wgbh/amex/three/

Three Mile Island Alert
  www.tmia.com

United States Nuclear Regulatory Commission's Students' Corner
  www.nrc.gov/NRC/STUDENTS/students.html

Further Reading

Virtual Nuclear Tourist
"Inside a Nuclear Power Plant"
www.nucleartourist.com/areas/areas.htm

"Three Mile Island Event"
www.virtualnucleartourist.com/events/tmi.htm

WashingtonPost.com
"Special Report: Crisis at Three Mile Island"
washingtonpost.com/wp-srv/national/longterm/tmi/tmi.htm

Videotapes

Gazit, Chana. *Meltdown at Three Mile Island.* 1999. Written and produced by Chana Gazit; edited and coproduced by David Steward. 60 min. WGBH Educational Foundation.

History Channel. *This Week in History*: "Three Mile Island." March 2001. Produced by Marc Etkind, Dan Levitt, and Julie Mirocha, with Pinball Productions. 60 min.

Index

Advanced Boiling-Water reactor, 113
Advisory Committee on Reactor Safeguards, 23, 37
Aircraft carriers, 25
Alpha decay, 19, 20
AmerGen, 98
AP600 reactor, 113
AP1000 reactor, 113
Arco, Idaho, nuclear power plant in, 28
Atom, 18
Atom bomb, 22, 24
Atomic decay, 18-19
Atomic Energy Acts, 23, 26, 31
Atomic Energy Commission, 23, 25-28, 29, 35, 37, 38-39, 44
Atomic mass number, 18
Atomic pile, 21

Babcock & Wilcox, 48, 63, 66, 73, 93, 94
Becquerel, Antoine Henri, 17
Beta decay, 19, 20
Bettis Atomic Power Laboratory, 25, 26
Boiling-water reactor, 23, 28, 32
BORAX III, 28
Bureau of Radiological Protection, 50, 61, 74, 76
Burns & Roe, 93

Carter, Jimmy, 56, 84, 86, 88, 98
China syndrome, 36-37
Cold War, 23-24
Control panel, 41-46, 50

Control rods, 15, 21, 42
Control valves, 14-15, 39, 42
Cooling towers, 14, 33
Curie, Marie and Pierre, 17

Dresden-1 nuclear power plant (Morris, Illinois), 34
Duquesne Light Company, 26

Eisenhower, Dwight D., 25, 26
Electricity, from nuclear plants, 12-13, 19-21
Electric Power Research Institute, 102-103
Electromatic relief valve, 14, 15, 42-43, 44, 45, 46, 47, 48, 94
Electrons, 18
Emergency core cooling system, 37-39, 43, 44, 45, 66, 73
Energy Reorganization Act, 38
Energy Research and Development Agency (Department of Energy), 38
Exelon, 113-114
Experimental Breeder Reactor, 23

Fast reactor, 31
Faust, Craig, 42, 43, 45
Fermi, Enrico, 19-22
Fission, 12-13, 15, 19-21, 32-33, 36, 46, 47
Frederick, Ed, 42, 43, 44, 45

Fuel rods, 12-13, 15, 32-33, 36, 64

Gamma rays, 20-21
Garnish, Holly, 12, 15
Gas-cooled reactor, 31
General Electric, 28-29, 34, 113
Generators, 13, 14, 15, 32, 41, 43, 45
Gray, Mike, 114

Hager, Robert, 115
Hahn, Otto, 19
Half-life, 19
Hiroshima, 22

Institute of Nuclear Power Operations, 103
Instrument air system, 14-15
International Energy Agency, 112
Isotopes, 18-19

Joint Committee on Atomic Energy, 25

Kemeny Commission, 98-99, 102, 103
Knolls Atomic Power Laboratory (Niskayuna, New York), 28
Kyoto Protocol, 114

Lead, 20-21
Light, Kari, 91-92
Loss-of-coolant accident, 36, 37, 44, 50, 94
Loss-of-Fluids-Test facility, 37

Manhattan Project, 22, 23, 28

Index

Metropolitan Edison
  and cleanup after disaster, 94-95
  and GPU as owner of, 98
  public mistrust of, after disaster, 103-104
  and public response to construction of Three Mile Island, 92
  and response to disaster, 48, 53, 59-61, 65-66, 68, 70, 77-78, 80, 88
  and safety of Three Mile Island, 93, 94
Military, nuclear power for, 22-25, 27
Miller, Gary, 50, 51

Nagasaki, 22
National Academy for Nuclear Training, 103
National Energy Security Act, 114
National Reactor Testing Station, 23, 28
Neutrons, 18
Nuclear chain reaction, 19-22
Nuclear Energy Electricity Assurance Act, 114
Nuclear power
  and legislation, 23, 26, 31, 114
  military uses of, 22-25, 27
  peacetime and commercial uses of, 22, 23, 24, 25-29. *See also* Nuclear power plants
Nuclear power plants
  electricity from, 12-13, 19-21, 23
  energy produced by, 112
  fission in, 12-13, 15, 19-21, 32-33, 36, 46, 47
  history of, 22, 23, 24, 25-29, 31-39
  location of, 35
  parts of, 12-13, 14
  and pollution, 35, 114
  and power-pooling, 35-36
  and safety after disaster, 112-114
  and safety before disaster, 32-33, 35, 36-39
  and turnkey contracts, 34-35
  types of, 12, 31-32, 113
Nuclear Regulatory Commission
  and Atomic Energy Act, 26
  on containment building in LOCA, 37
  formation of, 38
  and investigation of, into disaster, 102, 103
  and license for Three Mile Island plant, 98
  on nuclear plant construction, 34-35
  and response to disaster, 52, 53, 55-56, 61-62, 63, 68, 70, 74, 76, 78, 83-84, 88, 104
  and safety after disaster, 112-114
  and twelves, 42
  and WASH-1400, 38-39

Oyster Creek nuclear power plant (Toms River, New Jersey), 34, 93

Pebble Bed Module Reactor, 113-114
PEMA, 50, 51, 52, 56, 57, 74, 76, 78, 89
Pintek, Mike, 52-53, 60, 70, 78, 85
Pollard, Bob, 114-115
Polonium, 17
Power demonstration reactor program, 27-28, 31
Power-pooling, 35-36
Pressurized water reactor, 12-13, 14, 32, 93
Protons, 18

Radiation, 20
Radioactivity, 17-19
Radium, 17
Reactor building, 14
Reactor core, 13, 15, 33, 46-47, 48-49, 64
Rickover, Hyman, 24-25, 86
Roentgen, Wilhelm, 17
Rogers, Leland, 48
Rogovin Report, 102, 103

Scram (safety control rod axe man), 14-15, 21, 41, 46, 94
Scranton, Bill, 65, 68-70, 76, 84, 86, 92
Shippingport nuclear power plant (Pittsburgh), 26, 28, 29, 31-32, 33, 36
Strassman, Fritz, 19
Strauss, Lewis, 26
Submarines, nuclear, 25
System 80+ reactor, 113

Thermocouples, 48

Index

Thornburgh, Dick, 52, 71, 74-75, 76, 78, 80, 84, 86, 88, 89, 115
Three Mile Island disaster
and adverse health effects, 104-106
cause of, 13-15, 39, 42
chronology of events in, 41-51, 58, 64-65, 66-67, 78, 83-89
and cleanup, 94-98, 103
and computer, 46, 48, 49
and control panel, 41-46, 50
and evacuation, 74, 76-83, 86, 89, 115
and federal investigation, 98-99, 102, 103
federal response to, 55-56, 61-62, 63, 68, 74, 76, 78, 83-84, 86, 88, 91-92, 104-106
and future of nuclear power industry, 111-115
as general emergency, 51-53, 57, 60, 64
and hydrogen bubble, 64, 78, 83-89, 95
and jet of steam from Unit 2, 11-12, 15, 41
legacy of, 114-115
local meetings after, 91-92
local response to, 56-58, 65-66, 68-70, 80, 88
media reports of, 58-59, 65-66, 67, 68, 70-71, 76, 77, 78, 84-85, 115
and meltdown, 83-85, 95-97, 108
Met Ed's response to, 48, 53, 59-61, 65-66, 68, 70, 77-78, 80, 88
misinformation on, 57-63, 65-66, 68, 71, 74, 75-76, 78, 84, 85-88, 102, 103-104
and NRC investigation, 102, 103
and nuclear power industry reform, 102-103
and pregnant women and children, 78, 81-82, 115
public concerns after, 103-109
and release of radioactivity, 46, 47, 49-52, 58, 60, 61-62, 64, 65-66, 68-71, 73-75, 76, 77-78, 84-86, 104-108
and resumption of operations, 98
and safety, 14-15, 21, 32-33, 41-42, 61-62, 64-65, 94
and shutdown of plant, 98
as site emergency, 49-51
and warning to stay indoors, 74-75, 78
WKBO's announcement of, 52-53, 60
Three Mile Island power plant
cost of, 93, 94
history of, 11
parts of, 12-13, 14, 32
as pressurized water reactor, 12, 32, 93
problems with, 93-94
public reaction to, 92-93, 94
sale of, 98
Tokaimura, Japan, accident in uranium processing plant in, 111-112
Turbines, 13, 14, 15
Turnkey contracts, 34-35
Twelves, 42, 45

Uranium, 12-13, 17, 19-21

Vallecitos nuclear power plant (Pleasanton, California), 28-29, 31-33

WASH-1400 (Rasmussen Report), 38-39
Water-cooled reactor, 12, 31-32
Weinberg, Alvin, 22
Westinghouse, 113
Westinghouse Company, 21, 25, 26, 28, 34
Whittock, Bill, 11-12, 15
WKBO, 52-53, 60, 70-71, 78, 85
World War II, 22
Wydler, John, 68

X rays, 17

Zewe, Bill, 15, 41, 43, 45, 46, 48, 49, 50, 60

Picture Credits

page

2:	National Archives	43:	Associated Press, AP	81:	Jean DeAngelis
10:	© Wally McNamee/Corbis	47:	Associated Press, AP	87:	Associated Press, AP
14:	Jon DeAngelis	51:	Associated Press, AP	90:	Associated Press, AP
16:	© Digital Art/Corbis	54:	© Wally McNamee/Corbis	96:	National Archives
20:	Jon DeAngelis	59:	Associated Press, AP	97:	Associated Press, AP
24:	Bettmann/Corbis	62:	Roger Ressmeyer/Corbis	99:	Bettmann/Corbis
27:	Bettmann/Corbis	67:	Associated Press, AP	101:	Associated Press, AP
31:	© Charles E. Rotkin/Corbis	69:	Associated Press, AP	105:	National Archives
33:	World Nuclear Association	72:	National Archives	107:	National Archives
37:	Associated Press, AP	75:	©Leif Skoogfors/Corbis	110:	© Tim Wright/Corbis
40:	National Archives	79:	Bettmann/Corbis	115:	Bettmann/Corbis

Front cover: © Wally McNamee/Corbis
Back cover: © George Lepp/Corbis

THERESE DeANGELIS holds an M.A. in English literature and was a contributing editor for Chelsea House's Women Writers of English and Modern Critical Interpretations series. She has authored several books for young adults, including *Native Americans and the Spanish, Jodie Foster, New Mexico,* and *The Bombing of Pearl Harbor*; she also cowrote *Marijuana* in Chelsea House's Junior Drug Awareness series and *The Dust Bowl* in the Great Disasters series. The author grew up in Hershey, Pennsylvania, less than 10 miles from the Three Mile Island nuclear power plant; she now lives near Philadelphia with six funny little birds.

JILL McCAFFREY has served for four years as national chairman of the Armed Forces Emergency Services of the American Red Cross. Ms. McCaffrey also serves on the board of directors for Knollwood—the Army Distaff Hall. The former Jill Ann Faulkner, a Massachusetts native, is the wife of Barry R. McCaffrey, who served in President Bill Clinton's cabinet as director of the White House Office of National Drug Control Policy. The McCaffreys are the parents of three grown children: Sean, a major in the U.S. Army; Tara, an intensive care nurse and captain in the National Guard; and Amy, a seventh grade teacher. The McCaffreys also have two grandchildren, Michael and Jack.